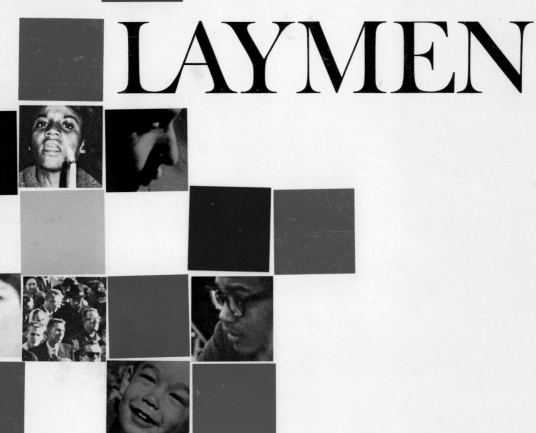

LAYMEN

VATICAN II's DECREE ON THE APOSTOLATE OF THE LAITY

with comment by:

Barbara Ward   Godfrey Diekmann

Yves Congar   Dan Herr

Dorothy Day   Dennis Geaney

Andrew Greeley   Mathew Ahmann   Mary Perkins Ryan

Michael Novak   Gerard Sloyan   Sister Charles Borromeo

                  Bishop Victor Reed

                  Dennis Clark   *and more than 60 others*

Introduction by Patrick Keegan

LAYMEN

Vatican II's Decree on the Apostolate of the Laity

**TEXT AND
COMMENTARY**

Edited by:
Peter Foote, John Hill, Laurence Kelly, John McCudden, Theodore Stone

Holt, Rinehart and Winston, Inc.

383 Madison Avenue, New York, New York 10017
Atlanta • Chicago • Dallas • San Francisco • Toronto • Montreal • London

Nihil Obstat: Rev. Edmund J. Siedlecki, S.T.D. Censor Librorum

Imprimatur: Most Rev. Cletus F. O'Donnell, J.C.D. Vicar General,
Archdiocese of Chicago

February 25, 1966

Photo credits:
JOHN ALHAUSER, pp. 15, 16, 47, 50
PAUL ALMASY, pp. 24, 40 (left)
FELICI, p. 4
FIDES PUBLISHERS, p. 13
ILLINOIS TOLLWAY, p. 9
VINCENT LOVETT, p. 48
SISTER MARY LUKE, S.S.N.D., p. 54
ROBERT McCULLOUGH, p. 8

NATIONAL CATHOLIC CONFERENCE
    FOR INTERRACIAL JUSTICE, pp. 10, 18
ROBERT NEWMAN, pp. 27, 34
JEROME RIORDAN, p. 40 (rt.), 44
ERNEST ROSENFELD, p. 32
KENNETH THOMPSON, p. 65
WESTRICH, p. 56
WIDE WORLD, pp. 36, 58

Design: GENE TARPEY

5806153

987654321

Preface

Among the stirring ideas of Vatican II was the idea of dialogue. The Council itself was a dialogue, a world-wide conversation among the Church's bishops. In addition to speaking with each other, they spoke with representatives of other Christian Churches, with members of non-Christian faiths, and with Catholic lay people, both men and women. On one historic morning in St. Peter's, the bishops listened to an English lay auditor, Patrick Keegan, speak to them about the layman's role in the Church. The exchange of views encouraged by Vatican II excited a listening world and refreshed the lives of millions.

In this spirit of dialogue, *Laymen* was written and published. It is something new in the field of Catholic publications. Before Vatican II, loyal Catholics felt that Church decrees were to be respected, assimilated, and implemented, but not judged or criticized. The new spirit of dialogue not only welcomes comment on the conciliar decrees but indeed calls for that comment. For how can the Church's full unity be realized if the bishops and their people are not free to speak with each other and comment on each other's views?

To get a good body of comment on the lay apostolate decree, an editorial team of laymen and priests wrote to the people whom they felt had the most to say about the lay apostolate. They invited each to write a brief comment about a particular article of the decree. Some who were invited to contribute to *Laymen* did not do so, and considerations of space prevented the editors from using all the material which was contributed. Nevertheless the editors have been impressed by the quantity and the overall quality of the contributions. Although they are grateful to all who have helped them to publish *Laymen*, they are especially grateful to the contributors.

THE EDITORS

Foreword

The Decree on the Apostolate of the Laity is an epoch-making document in the history of the Church. For the first time the apostolic activity of the laity is the object of a conciliar decree. It has been said that this decree consecrates all the achievements of the lay apostolate in the last forty years; it also ratifies most solemnly the task of the layman in the Church, the people of God.

It may be of some interest to outline briefly the history of the text of the Decree. Originally prepared by the preconciliar commission appointed by Pope John, this text did not come up for discussion until the Council's third session and meanwhile had been considerably refashioned, with increasing lay participation. The original version was seventy pages long; this was reduced first to forty-eight pages and then to fourteen by order of the Coordinating Commission, since part of the Decree's substance had been included in the Constitution on the Church and in "Schema 13"—The Church in the Modern World. The text was first discussed at the Council from October 7 to 13, 1964. It was my privilege at that time to act as spokesman for the laity and to speak to the assembled Council Fathers in a general congregation. It seems that this was the first time a lay voice had been heard in a general council since the days of the Emperor Constantine in 325 A.D!

The majority of the Council Fathers considered the text too clerical and juridical in its opposition of laity to Church, instead of the inclusion of the laity *in* the Church, as was done in the Constitution on the Church. This led to a new recasting during the intermission and this was voted on paragraph by paragraph from September 23 to 27, 1965. There was additional refashioning in accordance with the bishops' amendments and a new detail-vote took place on November 9, 1965. The final vote on the document as a whole was taken on November 10; only two votes were cast against the text.

The Decree cannot be considered on its own, but must be seen in the context of the great charter of the Council, *Lumen Gentium,* the Constitution on the Church. With this constitution the layman at last acquires a personality; he becomes an integral part of the people of God, with his own specific rights and responsibilities. The role of the layman in the mission of the Church here becomes soundly based on firm theological foundations and we see e end of the cleavage between clergy and laity at has been the source of so much confusion and many misdirected efforts in the past.

The Decree should also be read in conjunction ith the Declaration on Religious Liberty and the onstitution on the Church in the Modern World. s Father Congar has said: "These documents are full and frank recognition of the lay nature of resent society. The Church does not cease to teach ith authority but she enters into a dialogue with ankind, she outlines a theology of earthly reali-es; and she ascribes to lay people the specific and roper task of witness in the secular order and enewing that order." As the Decree states, in its econd article: "They must immerse themselves irectly and decisively in [the secular order], uided by the light of the Gospel and the mind of he Church, and motivated by Christian love."

It is a source of joy and happiness that the De-ree consecrates in the most solemn terms those atterns of the apostolate for which so many of s have worked; an apostolate that starts and is ooted in respect for the realities of human life; an postolate of like to like; a dynamic apostolate that elieves in using actual situations for formation hrough action, rather than training in a vacuum or hypothetical future action.

Inevitably, a document issued by the Church with er divine authority, but fashioned by human hands, ill be marked by imperfections. The chapter in he Decree on "The Various Types of the Aposto-ate," which consecrates all forms of apostolic en-eavor, is perhaps marked more clearly than any ther part of the Decree by the tensions of the Council and so fails to speak clearly about the na-ure of Catholic Action. Despite these unresolved ensions, which left the Decree taking an inter-ediary position, the document does not prevent he possibility of further clarification.

We may see, for example, that the lay apostolate ill one day give birth to movements of Christian nspiration informed by the spirit of the apostolate ut for which the Church will not be directly re-ponsible. This possibility is beginning to arise in ome countries now. Whatever happens, the dy-amism of such future developments will depend on he growth and influence of the movements of the ay apostolate, which are now accepted as fully be-onging to the Church's mission, providing these movements give a genuine formation that begins in actual life and is related to the real problems of people.

The article dealing with the coordination of the lay apostolate seems to presuppose an apostolic development at the base that may exist to some extent in a few European countries, but is by no means general elsewhere, particularly in the English-speaking countries. Before one coordinates there must be something of value to coordinate, otherwise there is the danger of the letter stifling the spirit. My own belief is that the prime need in English-speaking countries is to build at the grass-roots level apostolic movements concerned with promoting genuine commitment to earthly realities. Without such commitment, the apostolate has no substance and becomes a meaningless word.

All of us who have been involved in the lay apostolate through the years feel indebted to the priests who have sustained us spiritually in our commitment to our work in the modern world. A right relationship between priest and layman is indispensable for the implementation of this Decree. From experience we know that the basis of this cooperation is a mature relationship built on mutual trust and respect.

The Decree on the Apostolate of the Laity is a milestone on the path of the pilgrim Church. It is an act of trust by the Church assembled in Council in the apostolic potential of her people. All of us, as lay people, should be sobered by the thought that so far we have fallen short of the total apostolic commitment, in and through life, which the Church has now declared to be our duty and our privilege. Before the Council met we may have had some excuse for inaction, such as the lack of clarity in the layman's status. Such excuses can no longer be valid.

PATRICK KEEGAN

Contents

Decree on the Apostolate of the Laity

1.

Introduction

*T*his holy synod wishes to encourage a more intense apostolic activity by the whole people of God.[1] Therefore it begins now to consider with deep concern the role of those Christian faithful who are lay people. In previous Constitutions,[2] the synod has already declared that the place of lay Christians in the mission of the Church is an integral and altogether essential one. Their apostolate flows from the very calling to be followers of Christ and must always be present in the Church. Sacred Scripture itself clearly points out that in the earliest days of the Church the witness of lay people was quite spontaneous and markedly effective (see Acts 11:19-21; 18-26; Rom. 16:1-16; Phil. 4:3).

Our own age requires a similar zeal of lay people. Indeed the modern situation demands of lay people an even more intense apostolate, and one broader in scope. The accelerating population increase, the rapid advances of science and technology, the more intimate and complex relationships between peoples, all these have immensely broadened the range of the lay person's apostolate (in which there is generally no substitute for the lay person). Further, the factors mentioned have generated entirely new areas of concern which require expert attention and investigation by lay people. This kind of apostolate becomes all the more urgent because so many areas of human life have inevitably become extremely specialized. This specialization, in some instances, is accompanied by an alienation from moral and religious values, and consequent serious dangers to Christian living. In addition, without lay energies the Church could scarcely exercise its presence and ministry in the numerous places where priests are too few, or, as is sometimes the case, where priests are denied the freedom to minister.

This complex and pressing need for a vigorous lay apostolate is clearly signaled by the obvious action of the Holy Spirit today. More and more he awakens lay people to an awareness of their particular responsibilities in the Church and inspires them to dedicate themselves to Christ and his Church in every kind of service.[3]

In this decree, the Fathers of the Council will attempt to clarify the characteristics of the lay person's apostolate, its range and particular properties. They will also try to outline its basic principles and offer some pastoral suggestions for its more effective realization. Whatever is thus suggested should be looked on as proper legislation in the revision of canon law concerning the apostolate of lay people.

COMMENT

As article 1 points out, the modern world is a very complex, highly specialized and organized society. No one man, no one group of men, no matter how wise and competent, can know enough about the modern world to cope with its problems and offer guidelines for its integration into a meaningful and harmonious social pattern. For the modern world to feel the impact of the Gospel, the layman must make that Gospel applicable in the world. The layman must baptize our modern scientific, industrialized, mechanized society. By "baptize" we mean that he must render it human and meaningful, so that man can achieve both temporal and eternal felicity.

If the Church needs the layman to fulfill her mission on earth, because the laity is the people of God together with the clergy, it is also true that there are at present no structures, no guidelines to channel the activities of laymen into life-giving directions. There must be room for experimentation, room for initiatives coming from the laity and from lay-sponsored organizations. The time of a clerical monopoly on apostolic activity and apostolic direction passed with Vatican II.

Another point needs to be made. In the past the general conception of the apostolate implied that the laity was to help the priest in his work. This is still true of parish-based lay organizations. The Legion of Mary, for example, does good work as the long arm of the priest. The Confraternity of Christian Doctrine needs laymen and laywomen to staff catechetical centers. Such very important apostolic work will always be necessary.

But if the lay apostolate is to be principally concerned with the modern city, if it is to engage in social areas where the layman is at home, then the layman must be the principal agent of the apostolate and he will need the priest to help him with the spiritual tools appropriate to the lay state. This new orientation makes the layman responsible not merely for the carrying out of the apostolate, but even for the planning and structuring of it, always, to be sure, in close association with the Church's main source of responsibility, the bishops and the pope.

This constitutes the new challenge of the layman in the Church.

LOUIS J. PUTZ, C.S.C.

The decree on the apostolate of the laity affirms that it is the "whole people of God" who are called to "more intense apostolic activity." It is unfortunately true that this type of language says little or nothing to modern man. The language used in this Decree and generally by the Council is locked in the mold of yesteryear.

The Church comes close to the edge of a world dominated by "extreme specialization," and there the two, with great difficulty, try to communicate with each other in their specialized tongues. And at the last moment, the Church pulls back from this frontier and speaks out in the traditional and formal language of the past.

The world has changed more in the last twenty-five years than in all the rest of history combined and will change even more in the next ten years than in the last twenty-five years. It is at the center of action and change that the mission of the layman is to be exercised. He fashions his world to what God had in mind in the original spark of creation. It is by losing oneself in the task of seeking after justice that one finds himself. It is by plunging into the world that we will once again hear the word of God directing us to his Son, at the center of creation, so that together we can sing out the hymn of accomplished creation.

ROMEO MAIONE

I

The calling of the lay people to the apostolate

2.

On the share of lay people in the mission of the Church

*T*he destiny of the Church is to spread the kingdom of Christ over the whole planet and to enable all men to be saved and redeemed to the glory of God our Father.[1] Through men, the Church is to bring about a genuine harmony between the whole created order of the world and Christ. All the energies of the Mystical Body toward this goal are included in the term "apostolate." The Church carries out this apostolate through all her members, but in many different manners. The invitation to be a Christian is of its very nature a summons also to the apostolic mission of the Church.

Just as in biological structures each individual cell shares its own vitality with the life of the whole body, rather than being a passive component, so too in the body of Christ: his body is the Church, and the whole body "grows and builds itself up in proportion to the balanced activities of each one of the members" (Eph. 4:16). Indeed, the joint action and interrelation of the members in this body is so intimate that any single member who does not act to build up the Church according to his abilities must be said to do a disservice both to the Church and to himself (see also Eph. 4:16).

In the Church itself there is a unity of mission but many kinds of ministry. Christ gave to the apostles and their successors the task of teaching, sanctifying and governing in his own name and with his power. Lay people have also been made sharers in the priestly, prophetic, and royal office of Christ, and thus they exercise their proper role in the mission of the whole people of God, both within the Church and in the secular order.[2] They genuinely exercise the apostolate by their efforts to bring the news of the Gospel and the ways of holiness to mankind; they likewise exercise it by their efforts to permeate and perfect the secular order of things with the spirit of the Gospel. Thus their actions in this order will clearly witness Christ and work toward the salvation of mankind. It is the particular calling of lay people to be immersed in the secular world and its activities; and so they have a God-given vocation to cultivate a fervent Christian spirit and to act as a yeast in the secular order.

*For as the body is one and has many members, and
all the members of the body, many as they are, form
one body, so also is it with Christ (1 Cor. 12:12).*

COMMENT

The third paragraph of article 2 defines the place of the laity in the apostolate of the Mystical Body. First, a point of great importance is made: there is a unity of mission in the Church, but a diversity or plurality of ministries. We should rejoice at this return to the idea of ministries, in the plural, in contrast to the usage which for so long has reserved this term for the ministry of the priest alone. Laymen must be able to exercise true ministries in the Church, if their apostolic service is to have any kind of stability and is to be recognized in the Christian community.

This point made, the text goes on to distinguish, as one might expect, two main forms of the lay apostolate: the outright proclamation of Jesus Christ and his ways of salvation; and the exercise of an influence in and on temporal things, to order them toward God and according to God. This latter way is the *consecratio mundi*, which is not a "sacralization" by which temporal things are reclaimed from the area of the "profane" (an extremely ambiguous term which it would be much better never to use), but a sanctification of things through the good usage one makes of them. Laymen are both members of the people of God and active members of the earthly city. They are therefore able—in a way that no others are—to sanctify temporal realities from within. This is their own apostolate or, better, this is the form of the unique apostolate which is theirs.

As was said in the first paragraph of article 2, the Church, through men, through the faithful, tries to realize here below a certain unity, or at least a harmony, between the order of creation and Christ's work of salvation. The perfect unity of these two orders, however, will be achieved only in the eschatological Kingdom. Here below, even with the desire we have for His coming, we are able to trace out only imperfect, fragmentary, and obscure images of that final state.

YVES CONGAR, O.P.

The formulation found in this article certainly represents an advance over the former description of Catholic Action as "the participation of the laity in the apostolate of the hierarchy." The mission of Jesus is entrusted to the whole community, and it is the community that carries out the functions of teaching, ruling, and sanctifying. Thus every member of the Body of Christ is involved in the building up of the Body; some in a public manner, others privately. The layman exercises his mission on two different levels, that of evangelization and the level of the secular order. Properly speaking, the layman is one who takes the secular order seriously and it is here, generally speaking, that he carries out his responsibility to the mission of the Church or proves unfaithful to it.

JOSEPH DILLON

Over several centuries a process of centralization and clericalization has gradually disturbed the equilibrium which should exist among the various ministries of clergy, religious, and laity. The Decree undertakes to restore that equilibrium by focusing on the role of the laity in the Church's ecumenical adventure into the world. The laity are seen as the royal and prophetical priests of the secular, partakers of the reconciling priesthood of Jesus. To them belongs the ministry of social, political and economic reconstruction. Theirs is a work of service to the Gospel in the world of culture, a ministerial work which extends beyond the local and even the national into the international sphere.

The Christian is the servant of the good news of reconciliation proclaimed by Jesus; his vision must become truly planetary. And the lay Christian in an especial way is summoned to enter into this new perspective which St. Paul calls the mind of Christ.

DONALD P. GRAY

We find in this article that the vocation to the Church implies, as a consequence, the vocation to the apostolate. One cannot be a Christian without at the same time being an apostle. By the very fact of his being inserted into a harmonious and organic whole, every member of the Church is involved in and responsible for the good of the whole body. If he refuses to contribute to the good of the entire ecclesial organism, he is not helping either himself or the Church.

This concept implies that a member who does not contribute to the expansion of the whole body is a useless member and one whose presence actually constitutes a hindrance to the functioning and the vitality of the whole body.

This doctrine, on the one hand, disposes of the old way of looking at the laity as merely the "object" and not also the "subject" of the apostolate and, on the other hand, adds a new dimension to the Christian life. One cannot be a Christian, a member of the Mystical Body, without also having a role in the activity of the Church, in her efforts to spread the word of salvation and to acquire new brothers for Christ. Thus Christian existence, i.e. membership in the people of God, is not simply a passport to eternal life, but membership in a missionary organism which is destined to expand to the limits of the earth.

DOMENICO GRASSO, S.J.

3.
On the foundation of the lay apostolate

*L*ay people have a right and duty to exercise the apostolate which stems from their very union with Christ the Head. By baptism they are joined to the Mystical Body of Christ; they are strengthened by the power of the Holy Spirit in confirmation; and they are thus commissioned to the apostolate by the Lord himself. They are consecrated into the holy people of God and his royal priesthood in order that, through all their activities, they will be offering spiritual sacrifices and thus witness Christ through all the world. Through the sacraments, and especially through the Holy Eucharist, there is given and nourished within them that love which is the driving force of the whole apostolate.[3]

The apostolate should be carried out in that faith, hope, and charity which the Holy Spirit makes richly available to all members of the Church. Indeed it is by the precept of charity, the most important commandment of the Lord, that all followers of Christ are bound to work for the salvation of all men and to labor for the glory of God through the coming of his kingdom: so that they may know the only true God and his ambassador Jesus Christ (see John 17:3).

Therefore the foremost task of every faithful Christian is to pour out his energies so that the divine message of redemption may be heard and welcomed by all men everywhere.

The Holy Spirit works for the holiness of God's people through the sacraments and the service of ministry. To help them carry out their apostolate he also imparts to the faithful particular gifts which "he distributes among them just as he wishes" (1 Cor. 12:11), in order that "each one may use whatever endowments he has received in the service of others," and thus become himself "a good steward of the manifold bounty of God" (1 Pet. 4:10), for the building up of the whole body through love (see Eph. 4:16). By possessing these charisms, even the ordinary ones, there arises for each of the faithful both the right and duty to use them in the Church and in the secular order for the well-being of mankind and the growth of the Church. They are to be used in the freedom of the Holy Spirit who "breathes wherever he will" (John 3:8). They are to be used in mutual cooperation with all Christ's brothers, especially in cooperation with their pastors, whose duty it is to make judgment about the genuineness of these gifts and the disciplined use of them, not indeed "to extinguish the Spirit" (1 Thess. 5:19), but "to test all things and to hold on to that which is good" (1 Thess. 5:21).[4]

Even as thou hast sent me into the world, so I also
have sent them into the world (John 17:18).

COMMENT

One of the most far-reaching of recent theological "re-discoveries" is the link between baptism-confirmation and the apostolic mission of the Christian. Through these twin sacraments of Christian initiation a person is "ordained" to the service of the Church and of mankind. It cannot be underscored enough that an apostolic desire to communicate the good news of Christ to one's fellow-man is not a peripheral "extra" in the life of Christians. A confirmed man interested only in saving his own soul is no Christian at all. On the contrary, he is a caricature of what Christ intended his disciples to be. For he has been joined to Christ and from him has received the gift of the Holy Spirit.

Christ is the first "Apostle," that is, the One sent by God on a mission of universal salvation. What he has to give all men is the Holy Spirit, who alone can make us sons of God and brothers of one another. To have received the Holy Spirit, in however initial a fashion, and not to have been enkindled by the fire of divine love (he *is* love), is to have failed to respond to what one has become *in Christ*. If we are joined to Christ, as indeed we are, we are "marked men," identified with him in his apostolic zeal that cannot be quenched until the last man has had the chance to accept God's redemptive love.

FRANK B. NORRIS, S.S.

Perhaps one result of this Decree will be a decrease in the number of "lay apostles." And this will be all to the good. If every Christian is called to the lay apostolate, then what has seemed to many an exclusive society may be opened up to all people of God.

We are now told that the work of the lay apostolate can no longer be delegated to the committed few and we can no longer excuse our own failures by the plea that we have not been called to the higher life. It has been said that war is too important a matter to be entrusted to generals. It seems to me the Council Fathers are saying that the work of the lay apostolate is too vital to be left to "lay apostles."

Obviously, the issue is not that simple. Not only must all laymen be persuaded to take on the role of lay apostles, but pastors who are to make "disciplined use of them" must likewise be persuaded that the apostolic layman is not a busy-body and is not to be treated as a nuisance. This conversion, I suggest, will take a lot of persuading.

DAN HERR

4.
On lay spirituality in relation to the apostolate

*C*hrist, the ambassador of the Father, is the source and well-spring of the whole apostolate. Clearly then the effectiveness of the lay people's apostolate depends on their living in union with Christ, as the Lord himself said: "One bears abundant fruit only when he and I are mutually united; severed from me you can do nothing" (John 15:5). This life of intimate union with Christ is sustained within the Church by many kinds of spiritual assistance which are equally offered to all the faithful, the chief of which is active participation in the Sacred Liturgy.[5] These spiritual aids should be used so that lay people, by fulfilling their obligations to the secular order in their everyday lives, deepen their union with Christ through their secular work. That is the will of God for them. Certainly their union with Christ is not to be put into a separate compartment. With such an attitude lay people should have a prompt and cheerful spirit in their search for holiness of life, working to overcome obstacles in patience and wisdom.[6] Neither family responsibilities nor any other concerns of secular life should be extraneous to the conduct of their spiritual lives, as the Apostle Paul said: "Whatever you do or say, let it always be in the name of the Lord Jesus, while you give thanks to God the Father through him" (Col. 3:17).

Such a life will demand a persevering exercise of faith, hope, and love.

Only by the guidance of faith and reflection on the word of God can any man come to recognize in every moment and every place the God "in whom we live and move and have our being" (Acts 17:28). Only through faith and God's word can we seek out his will in our every decision, see Christ in every man, whether friend or stranger, and judge accurately the true meaning and value of secular realities both in themselves and in their relation to the final goal of man's life.

Those who possess such faith will live as sons of God, sure of the fulfillment of his revelation, and mindful always of the death and resurrection of the Lord. In this life's pilgrimage men of faith keep themselves from being enslaved to material affluence and, hidden with Christ in God, they turn their energies to enduring values; with a full and generous spirit they dedicate themselves to spreading the kingdom of God; they work to improve the secular order and to permeate it with a Christian spirit. Faced with the inevitable difficulties of life, they discover strength in Christian hope, counting "the sufferings of the present time as not worthy to be compared with the glory to come" (Rom. 8:18).

Inspired by that love which has its source in God, Christians do good to all men, especially to those who are of the household of the faith (see Gal. 6:19); they put aside "all malice, all deceit, hypocrisy, and envy, and all slander" (1 Pet. 2:1) and thus attract men to Christ. God's love is "poured forth in our hearts by the Holy Spirit who has been given to us" (Rom. 5:5) and enables lay people truly to express in their own lives the spirit of the Beatitudes. Because they follow Christ who was poor they are neither discouraged by poverty nor carried away by affluence; because they imitate the humble Christ they are not desirous of empty glories (see Gal. 5:26); they seek earnestly to please God rather than man, and they are always ready to abandon

(Continued on page 16)

COMMENT

This article assumes, quite rightly, that the living union of laymen with Christ is dependent on the measure in which the word of God is spoken effectively in their hearing. One cannot have lively faith in God, firm hope in the coming of his Son, or the love of his Spirit poured out in one's heart unless he has been addressed by the Father who will achieve the union of sons with his only Son. The following which Christ invites us to has as its condition renunciation, the shouldering of the cross. But this is a meaningless call if men are already destitute through circumstance and have nothing to renounce freely; if those who do the inviting in Christ's name are confused as to the goodness of matter, life, or work; if systematic efforts are not made to remove phrases like "the humble Christ" and "empty glories" from the category of religious cant and place them in a setting of Christian asceticism by teachers who know the difference between the two.

Article 4 of the decree names as the very condition of a life of the spirit for lay people the word of God spoken in a way so compelling that it invites reflection. This will be done, it assumes, through their taking part actively in the celebration of the liturgy. The liturgy is Christ's work which through meaningful sign becomes man's work. Laymen can "deepen their union with Christ through their secular work" if they see their life's task to be one and not two—if they are helped to identify this "secular work" as the very work of salvation.

Nothing can help them come to this realization, however, but forms of public prayer that express accurately the lives they live, the jobs they hold, the hopes and fears they experience. All

sacramental action is a testimony to faith. It must stand for a faith already held if it is to nourish faith still further. Liturgy is human behavior in a context of faith that must come out of the depths of human conviction. In the strictest sense imaginable liturgy is part of life.

Liturgy has not been part of life.

It has been a stylized version of prayerful behavior which once had meaning in the lives of those who prayed it. This meaningfulness has not been the case for centuries. Article 4 of the Decree rests foursquare on the assumption of new forms of public prayer in which liturgy speaks with the

accents of life. Christian life cannot be lived in the married, single, or widowed state without "honesty, the spirit of justice, integrity of life, courage, and a gentle regard for all men." The possibility of practicing these virtues depends directly on their being encountered with regularity in the Church's public sacramental prayer.

GERARD S. SLOYAN

According to its title, this article deals with lay spirituality *in relation* to the apostolate. It should be immediately apparent that it is dealing with lay spirituality, period, because the apostolate

(Continued on page 17)

everything else for the sake of Christ (see Luke 14:26), and to suffer persecution for the sake of conscience (see Matt. 5:10), mindful of the word of the Lord: "If anyone wants to become my follower, he must renounce himself and shoulder his cross; then he may be a follower of mine" (Matt. 16:24). They cherish a Christian friendship with one another, and no matter what hardships they face, they offer help to each other.

The spiritual life of lay people, described above in outline, ought to take its distinctive qualities from their marriage and family life, their single or widowed state, their conditions of health, and from their involvement in their own professional and social lives. They should be earnest then in cultivating the qualities and talents that fit these states in life, and they should make use of the gifts which they themselves have received from the Holy Spirit.

Beyond this, those lay people who, while following their lay calling, have joined one of the associations or institutes encouraged by the Church, should try faithfully to incorporate into their own spirituality the distinctive qualities proper to each association. They should also have high respect for professional competence, for a civic and familial sense of responsibility, and for the virtues particularly oriented to the social order: honesty, the spirit of justice, integrity of life, courage, and a gentle regard for all men; the genuinely Christian life cannot be lived without these.

The ideal model of this apostolic spirituality is the most blessed Virgin Mary, Queen of the Apostles. While on earth she lived a most ordinary life, busily working and caring for a family. Yet she was always united intimately with her Son and cooperated in an altogether unique manner in the work of the Redeemer. Now she has been assumed into heaven and with her maternal love concerns herself for the brothers of her Son who are still in pilgrimage, and involved in danger and difficulty until they arrive in their blessed fatherland.[7] All should venerate her with devotion and commend their lives and apostolates to her maternal care.

Whatever you do in word or in work, do all in the name of the Lord Jesus (Col. 3:17).

COMMENT

means one's entire life. And every Christian is an apostle. Sacral life and secular life are inextricable. Separating men's activities in those terms is merely an artificial separation for discussion's sake.

The article states that it is only an outline of lay spirituality. But one wonders whether this self-limitation excuses the lack of a more extended treatment of how spiritual and secular values are reconciled. Perhaps, though, we are all locked into the terms of the ancient debate which has been going on for two thousand years.

One teasing phrase is "the true meaning and value of secular realities both in themselves and in their relationship to the final goal of man's life." Directly following is the other half of the antithesis: "men of faith keep themselves from being enslaved to material affluence." With this "enslavement" following so closely on the "true meaning" of secular realities, there cannot be too much debate about the value of those realities. In fact, the question has been begged.

It seems that this article is less an outline for lay spirituality than a few suggestions about it. In seeking to be general it becomes rather simplistic and sometimes seem to base its conditions on the least common denominator: avoid vice, be virtuous.

If we are invoked to take up the Cross, if we must die before we rise again, we ought to be told a little more emphatically what our Cross is, what our death is today, in the modern world.

MR. AND MRS. JOSEPH BONSIGNORE

Christ is the source of our lives as Christians. Through faith and the sacraments, and especially through the Eucharist, we share in his saving death and resurrection. The Eucharist is not "a separate compartment," not merely a necessary *support* of our Christ-like life and apostolate: it is the source from which the latter proceeds, the foundation on which all is built. Our life and work as members and as ministers of Christ in the world are supposed to be the daily unfolding of the great "Amen" which we pronounce at Mass. And conversely, "the aim and object of apostolic works is that all who are made sons of God by faith and baptism should come together to praise God in the midst of his Church, to take part in the sacrifice, and to eat the Lord's Supper" (On the Sacred Liturgy, art. 10).

Another way of saying this: the Eucharist is our most important act of faith, hope, and charity. By our participation in the Mass, we "proclaim the death of the Lord" (faith); we join with our heavenly family in worship and receive "the food of immortality," "the seed of resurrection" (hope); and we, "though many, become one body, by partaking of the one bread" (charity). Our article (and the entire Decree) then spell out how these virtues of faith, hope, and charity should become fully operative in apostolic action.

GODFREY DIEKMANN, O.S.B.

II

The goals to be achieved

5.

Introduction

Christ's work of redemption is directed both toward the salvation of men as individuals, and at the renewal of the whole secular order. Hence the Church's mission is not only to preach Christ and his grace to men, but also to bring the secular order to perfection by permeating it with the spirit of the Gospels. Therefore lay people in carrying out this mission of the Church will exercise their apostolate both in the life of the world and within the Church, in both the sacred and secular orders. These two orders, though they are quite distinct from one another, are so bound together in God's one providence, that God himself clearly seeks in the work of Christ, to gather up all the created universe in a new creative act, which is begun in time and brought to fulfillment in eternity.

COMMENT

Our redemption cannot be reduced to Christ's crucifixion nor is it simply preaching to men *about* Christ and supernatural grace. The Church's true mission is much broader in scope. Christ is the Word of God, Love made flesh. Hence to preach Christ fully means to give flesh to divine love in every phase of daily life.

As the Mystical Body of Christ the Church is the fulfillment of Bethlehem's promise; it is the necessary extension of that prototype incarnation of divine love in our temporal universe. Thus conceived, the mission of Christ and his Church is a cosmic task that will be completed only at the Parousia, when everything and everyone in our universe should be transparent (transfigured) by selfless love. This is the fulness of the Epiphany: a truly cosmic incarnation of God, the divine diaphany in which love shines forth from the heart of all matter, a cosmic transubstantiation or "transignification."

Separations of the natural and supernatural, of the secular and religious have meaning only for the compartmentalizing minds of idealistic philosophers. For those who take the Incarnation seriously and know how to unveil Christ hidden in all things, nothing in this world can be profane. This new emphasis and appreciation of the priesthood of the laity demands a total re-evaluation of the clerical state and the role of ordained priests. Thus we will better understand the Church as God's people, "the Catholic faithful, all who believe in Christ, and indeed the whole of mankind [who] belong to or are related to it in various ways" (Constitution on the Church, art. 13).

ROBERT T. FRANCOEUR

For too many centuries, leaders in the Church have stressed the eternal to the practical exclusion of the Christian obligation to time, to the secular order, to the concerns and needs of the entire material world. We are asked now to give this world its due by positive action in it, and we are asked to do so as Christians. The stress is on time rather than on eternity, for although both the secular and sacred orders are logically distinct, the secular has a certain preeminence in the order of work and actual concern. The startling importance of the Incarnation is that the Word comes in time to the world. The work is done *here*.

This introduction to chapter II, however challenging and refreshing, does contain an underlying ambivalent attitude. The chapter opposes the secular to the sacred, yet we would be hard put to imagine any man capable of living solely in the sacred order. Throughout the chapter one often finds the people of God placed in opposition to God's total creation.

The Christian is at home in the world by virtue of the mystery and grace of the Incarnation. The Incarnation fused the sacred with the profane. Jesus of Nazareth, the Christ, worked in time and in the world and those who follow him are the Church. I should hope that the practical implementation of this document will further clarify the essential message of the Incarnation, where Word and world, the sacred and the secular, are one in time, and where the Christian works within this integrated whole.

DAVID L. McMANUS

6.

The apostolate of spreading the gospel and sanctifying men

*T*he Church's mission is concerned with man's salvation, which is to be achieved through faith in Christ and by his grace. Therefore the apostolate of the Church and of all its members is principally directed toward witnessing Christ to the world by word and action, and by serving as a channel of his grace. This is done primarily through the ministry of word and sacrament which has been entrusted in a special way to the clergy. However lay people have their own important part to play in this ministry, too, so that they may become "fellow-workers for the truth" (3 John, 8). On this level particularly, the apostolate of lay people and the pastoral ministry mutually complement one another. Lay people have innumerable opportunities for the apostolate of evangelizing and sanctifying. The very witness of a Christian life and good works done for a supernatural motive powerfully attracts men to faith in God, as the Lord says: "Let your light shine before your fellow men, that they may see your good example and praise your Father who is in heaven" (Matt. 5:16).

However, this kind of apostolate is something more than just good example; the true apostle seeks out opportunities of preaching Christ, sometimes by leading non-believers toward faith, sometimes by instructing the faithful themselves, strengthening them, and stimulating them to a more dedicated life. "Love for Christ drives us on" (2 Cor. 5:14). The hearts of all believers should echo with those words of the Apostle Paul: "Woe betide me if I do not go on preaching the gospel" (1 Cor. 9:16).[1]

Further, our times witness the rise of new doubts. We are threatened by quite dangerous errors which are working to overturn religion, the moral order, and human society itself. Because of them, this holy synod heartily exhorts lay people to be even more earnest in the explanation, defense, and application of Christian principles to the problems of our day. Naturally they will do this, each in the light of his own talents and understanding, and in accord with the mind of the Church.

Let your light shine before men, in order that they
may see your good works and give glory to your
Father in heaven (Matt. 5:16).

COMMENT

In this article the Council Fathers hasten to make very clear that the contribution of the laity in spreading the Gospel is not merely accessory or provisional. It is characterized explicitly as important and as the laity's "own," i.e. a part which cannot be substituted by the clergy; the text speaks of mutual completion.

The Council wishes to destroy the prevalent and wrong opinion which sees in the catechetical contribution of the laity an extension or replacement for the clergy, when the latter cannot do the job. Even where an abundance of excellently trained clergy is available, the catechetical contribution of the laity is not only desirable, but necessary. It consists above all in the testimony of the Christian life they lead in their homes and in the communities to which they belong. Modern catechetics stresses "the testimony of Christian living" as one of the four main ways to transmit the Christian message from generation to generation. It is understood above all as the testimony of the community—the family, parish and so on—which has a very special formative power.

Everywhere lay Christians have many opportunities to do something more than just give a good example. They have countless opportunities for their apostolate of the word which are proper to them, e.g., the formation of children by parents after Christ, the apostolate of the encouraging and enlightening word in dealing with friends, neighbors, and fellow workers. The true lay apostle will not only seize opportunities which offer themselves, but will seek and find them. Is it not significant that Mother Church in this connection applies to lay Catholics the strong words of St. Paul: "Woe to me if I do not preach the gospel"?

JOHANNES HOFINGER, S.J.

Basic to an understanding of the fact that "the apostolate of lay people and the pastoral ministry mutually complement one another," is the honest recognition of the laity's essential function in the *priestly* people of God. The Church's primary work of witnessing Christ by serving mankind through the ministry of word and sacrament cannot be done without the genuine participation of lay people.

Perhaps one expression which has clouded our understanding not only of the priestly action of the laity, but of the sacramental action itself is that of "channeling grace."

"Communicating" rather than "channeling" might help express the reality of the Church's priestly action more accurately and clearly. Communication involves persons; it necessitates listening; it evokes response. Communication between the divine Persons and men means life, because it is love in action, love expressed.

In continuing the communicating of the Word of the Father, Jesus Christ our Lord, his Christians speak with him of the limitless love and deep concern of their heavenly Father. This speaking is done often by action, because men have always understood that actions speak louder than words. But just as the choice of words is important in communicating a message of genuine love, so too is the choice of action. A "supernatural motive" will always be significant, but when it is accompanying a good work which is not wisely chosen and carefully executed, it cannot speak well of our Father's love for mankind now, a love which is meeting the real needs of real people. As "love of Christ impels us" (2 Cor. 5:14), better ways to speak meaningfully the "good news" of Christian love must be discovered. This discovery process

will be largely the work of the priestly laity immersed in the mainstream of human life.
SISTER MARY CAROL FRANCES, B.V.M.

Infusing Christ's transforming power into secular affairs is indispensably the task of the layman. In pursuing this task, he is called upon to be both scientist and artist.

As scientist, he grasps the meaning of the Christ-event in history. He sees the world awaiting redemption. He distinguishes its redeemable elements from the unredeemable. He achieves spiritual maturity not in flight from the world, but rather in and through the world. He realizes that he is an imitator of Christ, but, more importantly, a member of Christ making present the reality of Christ in each life-situation, in each confrontation with another.

As artist, he is called upon to adapt Christ's presence to unique circumstances of time and place. In word and action, he must assert the primacy of the spiritual in the temporal order, particularly in a rising tide of affluence. This requires keen observation, prayerful reflection, detachment, and courage.

Tensions between Christian and non-Christian values reach their most agonizing stress in the experience of the layman. This is at once his great hardship and opportunity; for in the resolution of these tensions there issues personal spiritual progress, along with an integrated set of values, both Christian and non-Christian, which he alone can transmit to society.

EDWARD C. BURKHARDT

7.

On renewing the secular order in a Christian way

*G*od's plan for the universe calls for men, working harmoniously together, to renew the secular order and continuously improve it.

All that makes up the secular order, goods and property, family values, the economic order, the arts and professions, political institutions, international relations and other similar realities, together with their development and advancement, are not merely means to assist man toward his final goal. They have a validity of their own. That validity is established in them by God, and holds whether you look just at each one in itself or see them as components of the whole secular order: "And God looked at all which he had created, and they were indeed good things" (Gen. 1:31). To this natural goodness of the created order is added a certain special dignity because of its relation to the human person, for whose service it was created. Finally, it pleased God to bring together in one person, Jesus Christ, all realities, both natural and supernatural, "so that he may have pre-eminence over every creature" (Col. 1:18). This ordering of things, however, does not strip the secular order of its own independence, its own goals, laws, tools, and importance for human welfare. Rather the secular order is thus perfected in its natural excellence and brought into harmony with the whole vocation of man here on earth.

In the course of history the handling of things in the secular order has been attended by serious abuses. That is because men, under the influence of original sin, have frequently fallen into a host of errors about the true God, the nature of man, and the principles of the moral law; thus morality and human institutions were corrupted, and frequently the human personality itself was held in contempt. Indeed many men of our own times, because they are overly impressed by advances in science and technology, tend to a sort of worship of the material order, thus making themselves slaves rather than masters of it.

It is the task of the whole Church to help enable mankind to harmonize the entire order of secular realities, and direct it toward God through Christ. It is the duty of pastors to explain clearly the principles concerning the purpose of creation and the use of material things, and to offer the spiritual and moral supports needed to renew the secular order in Christ.

But lay people must take the renewal of the secular order as their own proper task. They must immerse themselves directly and decisively in it, guided by the light of the Gospel and the mind of the Church, and motivated by Christian love. They must work as citizens together with other citizens, each person with his own specific competence, and his own proper responsibility; and their goal must be to seek always and in all matters the justice of the kingdom of God. The secular order must be so renewed that, without violence to the integrity of its own laws, it is brought into harmony with the deepest principles of Christian living, and made to conform to the human needs of our varying localities, times, and peoples. Principal among the tasks of this apostolate is the social action of Christians, which this holy synod today desires to see extended to the whole range of temporal realities, and especially to the advancement of the intellectual order.[2]

For every creature of God is good, and nothing is to be rejected that is accepted with thanksgiving (1 Tim. 4:4).

COMMENT

From this article it would seem that the Council Fathers are visualizing all men, of all nations, from all vocations, professions, and classes, working together to gear all institutions to the maximum benefit of mankind and its needs.

Such institutional renewals are not to be carried out by organizations parallel to those already existing, or by blessing with holy water those of non-aligned religious basis, but rather by respecting individuals and institutions for their own worth, and by enhancing their good goals with our own efforts wherever and whenever accepted.

Our greatest weakness in the Church is our failure, through sermons, and other educational means, to make the layman realize that it is through the secular order that he must live and become a son of God. Unless bishops, pastors, and the clergy take some affirmative action in educating themselves in the economic facts of life, the influence of mass media, urbanization, racial justice, international trade, civic life, the U.N., unions, slum clearance, technology, cybernetics, etc. their words will never stimulate the laymen to action, and the Church will remain only buildings.

If priests could only accept the fact that laymen are not inferior to them, but simply have a different function to perform in the Mystical Body, there would be no need for decrees on the apostolate of the laity. Many priests may still have a better education than their contemporaries who are laymen. But to realize that laymen have superior knowledge and expertise in many fields only touched by generalities in seminary training is the first humble step that every pastor and bishop has to make to bring any of the Council's decrees into meaningful existence.

ANTHONY ZIVALICH

It is cause for rejoicing that the Church here explicitly recognizes the worth of the secular order as such, and that it states so clearly that all lay people have a positive duty to work to renew it and improve it. One can hardly imagine the shift in emphasis in religious education and in vocational counselling given under Catholic auspices, which should result from taking this article seriously.

Yet this article does not make it sufficiently clear, it seems to me, that the renewal and improvement of the secular order mean making it more human, more conducive to the personal and social development of human persons in society. The end of the last paragraph suggests this, but the phrase "to renew the secular order in Christ" might seem to mean something else. A great deal more thinking needs to be done as to what "reestablishing all things in Christ" really means as a guide to action.

Also, while lay people should "take the renewal of the secular order as their proper task," it should be recognized that priests and religious are citizens, with the same obligations as citizens that lay people have. And, to the extent to which the institutional Church is actually involved in the secular order, through ownership of property, employment, etc., "pastors" must be doing more than explaining principles and giving spiritual and moral support to lay efforts; they must be acting to renew the social order also, or lay efforts will be largely futile.

MARY PERKINS RYAN

It is improper to speak as if God has "a plan" for what will happen in the United States ten years hence, let alone for the whole universe. God's knowing, willing, and doing are simultaneous with the entire course of history; contingent things happen contin-

gently, free decisions are taken freely, singular events retain their uniqueness and their happenstance. Consequently, men are more free within history and responsible for planning the course of history than this article suggests. God does not plan history before men do.

Again, there are no purely "natural" realities. "Natural" is an abstract term, a possible but not actual line of reference. There never was nor will there ever be a purely natural man. Every man is in fact, whether he recognizes it or not, involved in the fall and the redemption. Consequently, a complete contrast between *"realities,* both natural and supernatural," is fallacious. There is only one concrete, real world. Every reality is, in the concrete, both secular *and* sacred, natural *and* supernatural. There are not "two" worlds.

In general, this article too easily assumes that the secular order, "without violence to the integrity of its own laws" can be "brought into harmony with the deepest principles of Christian living." It does not adequately recognize the ravages of self-interest and the will-to-power which characterize men in history, both secular and ecclesiastical. A more accurate statement of the relation between the secular and the supernatural is that, "while sin abounds, grace abounds even more." Every single object, event, and person in the world is, in the concrete, both subject to ordinary laws, contingencies, and sin, and also redeemed and symbolic of redemption. Everything is secular; but grace, as well, is everywhere.

MICHAEL NOVAK

8.

On works of charity as the hallmark of the Christian apostolate

*E*very work of the apostolate should be founded in charity and from charity draw its strength. Yet some particular works are by their very nature capable of giving a more striking witness of love. Christ our Lord wished such works to be the signs of his messianic mission (see Matt. 11:4-5).

The greatest commandment of the law is to love God with our whole hearts, and to love our neighbor as ourselves (see Matt. 22:37-40). Christ made this command of love for neighbor his own, and enriched it with a new dimension when he identified himself with all his brothers as the object of our charity, teaching us: ''as long as you did it for one of these least brothers of mine, you did it for me'' (Matt. 25:40). For he, by taking on a human nature, gathered all mankind into a kind of supernatural and familial solidarity with himself and established love as the mark of his followers when he said: ''by this token all the world must know that you are my disciples, that you have love one for another'' (John 13:35).

By coming together at the *agape* of the eucharistic banquet, the holy Church in her early days demonstrated that her members were united around Christ in the bond of charity. In the same way she is recognizable in every era by this outward sign of love. Thus, while

(Continued on page 26)

By this will all men know that you are my disciples,
if you have love for one another (John 13:35).

COMMENT

The absolute obligation of all followers of Christ to practice the works of mercy, which are called in this article the works of charity, is emphasized in the twenty-fifth chapter of St. Matthew, and indeed we will be judged as to whether or not we have given food to those who are hungry, sheltered those who have been deprived of shelter, clothed the naked, visited the sick, the prisoner, and shown respect for the dead by giving them proper burial. All these works of love are physical, and through them we recognize the Incarnation of our Lord, and show our love and gratitude to him for becoming one of us, showing us the way to a new life, and nourishing us to strengthen us for it.

Father Jimmy Tompkins of Nova Scotia said once that all our work, by which we earn our living by the sweat of our brow, also reflects the creativity of God. We become co-creators with him, and should reflect some aspect of this mercy, this love. In other words work should be for the common good, to enrich the body and mind and spirit so that we can grow in love. Works of charity should begin with ourselves, with a sense of personal responsibility to calls made upon us so that we each contribute what we can, even though it be only the widow's mite which Jesus praised so highly. Whatever we give will be increased as he increased the loaves and fishes of the little boy on the hillside who thus helped to feed the multitude.

Of course we help impersonally by our taxes too, but it is startling to know that only 12 per cent go for health, education, and works of charity and foreign aid, whereas 65 per cent are earmarked for the prosecution of the war in Vietnam, and for "defense" spending.

But are works of war compatible with works of love, of charity? "You know not of what spirit you are," Jesus said to his Apostles when they wished to call down fire from heaven on the inhospitable Samaritans.

A retreat master once said to us, "You love God as much as the one you love the least." Only the Holy Eucharist can teach us, by enabling us to grow in love, and from love, in understanding, these not so simple demands of charity.

DOROTHY DAY

For two thousand years the Church has carried forward the visionary ideal of humanity as a single family under the fatherhood of God, of a human unity so close that it can only be compared with the union of members in a single body, of branches on a single vine. But today this is not a vision. Physically, technically, it is a fact. By television, by satellite, by supersonic plane, we live in the closest physical contact—almost as we might live in a family. But there the resemblance ceases. For, across our narrow frontiers, we lack family love. We lack family obligation.

The scale of our obligations can be measured by the fact that the white, post-colonial, post-Christian minority who live in North America and Europe consume each year over 70 per cent of the world's wealth, although they make up less than 20 per cent of the world's people. They absorb over 70 per cent of the world's investment and conduct over 70 per cent of its trade. Each year their wealthiest member—the United States—*adds* to its national income more than the equivalent of *all* the resources of Africa or India. This addition—which in 1965 amounted to $47,000 millions—equals more than half of all the resources available to Latin America.

This is the scale of the gap between rich nations and poor nations. This is the scale of our international obligations not so much in charity as in justice. Nor can we doubt, if as wealthy Christians we evade this responsibility, that the divine judgment passed on Dives will fall on us for our neglect of our brother Lazarus, sitting hungry at the Western gate.

BARBARA WARD

Article 8 of this Decree is very clear, but I would like to bring special attention to three points.

First: charity must be fulfilled toward every man, regardless of race, color, or creed, and not only to Catholics or to people of our own race, parish, or country. Charity is love, and love is universal.

Second: charity cannot be mixed with the idea of proselytism or conversion. We should help someone because this person is another human being, poor or in need, and because this person is Christ on earth. There should be no other motives behind our charitable gestures.

Third: one should practice charity with munificence. If we really believe that Christ is present in the poor, then nothing should be too nice, too good, or too expensive for the poor—Christ. Too often we think charity to the poor is giving them only a piece of bread, a bowl of soup, or some used, unwearable clothing. But even the poor need something else

(Continued on page 27)

she rejoices in the charitable undertakings of others, she does claim the works of charity as her own duty and right which cannot be taken from her. For this reason our Church gives a special place of honor to mercy for the sick and needy, to the works of charity, and to mutual aid for the relief of every type of human need.[3]

In our time these activities and works are universally more urgent, for geographical distances have been shrunken, communication between men made more instantaneous, and the inhabitants of the whole planet have become, as it were, simply the members of a single family. Our charitable activity today can and ought to include every single member of the human family, and all his needs. Wherever people are poorly fed, clothed, housed, lack medical care, employment, education and the facilities for living a genuinely human life, wherever they are tormented by hardship or illness, wherever they suffer exile and imprisonment, there precisely should Christian charity be present, seeking them out and finding them in order to comfort them with its deep concern and support them with the help it offers. This obligation rests primarily on those individuals, and nations who are themselves prosperous.[4]

So that no one may be excluded from this kind of love, and that its universality be sharply evident, let us see in our neighbor the likeness of God, to whose image he has been created, and the person of Christ the Lord, to whom in reality is offered whatever is given to the needy; let us respect with the greatest gentleness the personal dignity and freedom of those we help; let the purity of our intention be unsoiled by any seeking for our own advantage, or any search for power;[5] let us first satisfy the demands of justice and not offer as the outpouring of charity what is already owed under the claim of justice; let us eliminate the causes of distress, not merely its symptoms; and let us so manage our assistance that those who receive it will gradually be freed from dependence on others and become capable of helping themselves.

Lay people then must greatly respect the works of charity and devote their energies to them. They should cooperate with all men of good will in supporting the undertakings of "social welfare" both public and private and also international aid, by which effective assistance is made available to individuals and to nations.[6]

COMMENT

than a bowl of soup to brighten their lives. If God permitted men to have modern comfort and luxury, it is against nature to think this comfort and luxury should be reserved to a certain privileged category of people. It should also be offered to the poor whenever there is an occasion.

MICHAEL SALMON

A striking feature of this article is the notion that we no longer know the poor and the suffering, and therefore must go and seek them out in order to comfort them. Indeed each one of us is poor, but the poverty of affluence seems to have an element of choice or self-creation. The luxury of freedom is not present for the economically impoverished. We who are affluent must learn to listen, and learn to give of ourselves more freely, without reserve. For many this will be difficult. It means the scales must fall from our eyes. We must begin to be unafraid. Then we may experience the solidarity of all men. And our response may "include every single member of the human family, and *all* his needs."

There are many pitfalls to a term like "works of charity," for too many seem to view the Christian apostolate as something limited. Fortunately, we have a way out of the malaise of this ambiguous terminology. First satisfy the demands of justice and recognize what is already owed under this claim. I believe this to be the most significant point of this article. Justice offers an opportunity for the newly reborn Christian as well as for many who have been willing but unsure as to where to start. Justice ties men together in their mutual poverty. We must turn toward one another to begin our activity of reconciliation and re-creation.

JERRY CHARIPAR

The concept of international justice is sadly lacking among national and church leaders in the United States. Many of our national leaders, not excluding some presidents, have said that the United States has absolutely no responsibility *in justice* toward the pressing needs of the poorer nations. National interest often is then the only criterion for determining American involvement or non-involvement in the international scene.

Unfortunately, the voice of the Catholic Church in the United States has been loudly silent on the question of justice between nations. It is a time in which very little has been written about international justice by moral theologians. However Catholic leaders cannot use this as an excuse for their silence.

The essential responsibility *in justice* of "rich nations" toward poorer nations is quite clearly outlined by Pope John in *Mater et Magistra* and *Pacem in Terris*. A major reason for this silence seems to be that international social justice is a very hot subject, especially among the substantial benefactors to the brick-and-mortar projects of our dioceses, parishes, and religious orders.

The practical ramifications inherent in international social justice are perhaps the acid test for bishops, pastors, and individual Catholics regarding authentic acceptance of collegiality. A list of these ramifications would include:

1. The sending and supporting of United States personnel for service in foreign countries.

2. Material support for native-born foreign citizens and programs in other countries.

3. Increased socio-economic assistance to the materially poorer nations.

4. An initiative to create those judicial world structures which recent popes have stressed as necessary for a just and equitable peace and for cooperation in our interdependent world.

GERALD F. MISCHE

III

On the various areas of the apostolate

9.
Introduction

*L*ay people exercise their diversified apostolate in the Church and in the secular order. On both levels there are a variety of areas for apostolic action, of which we wish to mention here the more important. They are: Church communities, the family, youth, the social environment, the nation, and the international community. Further, in our times women have an increasingly larger role in the life of society; it is then quite important that they participate more intensively also in the various areas of the apostolate.

10.
Church communities

*B*ecause they are partners in the priestly, prophetic, and regal role of Christ, lay people share actively in the life and action of his Church. Within the communities of the Church, their cooperation is so much needed that without it the apostolate of the pastors would be largely ineffectual. Like the men and women in the Gospel who assisted Paul (see Acts 18:18-26; Rom. 16:23) lay people with a genuinely apostolic attitude make up for what their brothers lack, and refresh the spirit of pastors and fellow faithful alike (see 1 Cor. 16:17-18). They themselves are strengthened by sharing actively in the liturgical life of their own community, and are prompt to take part in its apostolic efforts; they attract back to the Church those who have fallen away; they cooperate earnestly in presenting the teaching of God, particularly by catechetical instruction; by offering their own competences they lend added efficiency to the care of souls and even to the management of Church properties.

The most obvious example of the community apostolate is the parish. Here a wide variety of people are gathered together in one assembly and united with the Church universal.[1] We desire that lay people in the parish work in close cooperation with their priests,[2] that they bring to this assembly of the Church their own problems and the questions of the world relating to salvation, for common study and resolution; and finally we hope that they will lend their energetic assistance to every apostolic and missionary program of this, their ecclesial family.

At the same time they should have an appreciation of the diocese, of which the parish is a cell, as it were. They should readily lend their energies to diocesan programs too, at the invitation of their bishop. Indeed the needs of both urban and rural areas today[3] require that lay collaboration be extended outside the parish and diocesan territory to embrace the inter-parochial, inter-diocesan, national, and international levels. This is all the more needed because the increasing mobility of people, and the parallel speed of communication and growing closeness between segments of society no longer allow any one segment to be self-contained. And so they should be concerned for the needs of God's people over the whole range of the planet. Missionary works then, through the contribution of material and even personal assistance, are of special importance. For it is the Christian's duty and privilege to return to God a portion of the bounty received from Him.

While we have time, let us do good to all men, but especially to those who are of the household of faith (Gal. 6:10).

COMMENT

Since it is the Eucharist which is *the* event which God's people are called to celebrate as an assembly, it follows that the primary test of the parish as a community should be the Sunday eucharistic service. Only rarely do we find a people who are aware of their oneness in Christ as they worship communally. The new liturgical forms have failed to break through the hard shell of theological individualism which centuries of preaching and practice have formed and which protects people from coming too close to each other in a worshipping community.

A eucharistic community must express itself in witness and service. Again our traditional parish societies are hardly effective forms for a community apostolate. They were shaped in and for an immigrant ghetto-Catholicism. The age of pluralism and ecumenism demand new forms for a parish, or localized witness and service. If the parish is to become an obvious example of a community apostolate, new structures must be created which make the parish responsive to the theology of the Constitution on the Church and to the sociological realities of metropolitan or urban culture.

The decree on the lay apostolate is more a historical document than a blueprint for the future. It is a point of departure for people on the frontiers. The living Word in the world and the Church move on while the documents of Vatican II recede into history.

DENNIS J. GEANEY, O.S.A.

All talk of working on interparochial, inter-diocesan, national, and international levels is futile unless the concrete, genuine problems of parishioners can be dealt with in the parish life and liturgy.

Under present conditions, this is impossible. Parishes have not been structured with this end in mind. Their size has been determined largely by the demands of physical facilities. (A parish is "split" when it has too many people for the existing facilities, but enough people to finance new ones.)

What are the optimum size, character, and communal and liturgical activities for a parish which wants to make its lay persons' "own problems and the questions of the world" central to its life and worship? It will take sociology, psychology—maybe even economics and political science!—to find out. At any rate, such a parish would be considerably different than the ones we know today.

The language of article 10 is unexceptionable: no catchphrases here. The fact is almost hidden that, if this article is to be taken seriously, the structure and life of American parishes must be radically revised.

PETER STEINFELS

The apostolate of the laity is the working out in practice of the gifts of the Holy Spirit. These are never given only for individual sanctification. As a cell in the body of the whole Christ, the individual participates in the whole life of Christ, in his own soul, in the parish, in the diocese, in the whole Church. The intelligent layman must seek to understand and willingly engage in the entire apostolate. Jesus said that it was a sin to bury one's talents.

BISHOP STEPHEN A. LEVEN

We are so parish-oriented that the more apt description of our present posture is *parochial* rather than *catholic*.

The incisive question for the present and the future is this: How can the principle of subsidiarity be applied to Church communities? Specifically, what in the present parish structure is adequate? What are the parish's limitations? To what extent are meaningful structures needed at the inter-parish, inter-diocese, national and international levels? How will these be created, both as formative structures and as viable means of action? For this world no longer allows "any one segment to be self-contained. And so they should be concerned for the needs of God's people over the whole range of the planet."

The chief asset that lay people bring to the apostolate is their secularity, their at-one-ness with this world which needs Christ's redeeming grace. This last paragraph in article 10 hints at but does not resolve one of the major problems facing Church communities. They no longer fit the secular organization of this world. In the Church, in the apostolate, the layman operates within one framework; the real life out there, the secular life in which he works and lives is very different.

The decree treats the present canonical parish usually territorial, both as a source of apostolic formation and grace, and as a legitimate vehicle for lay action. Without question there is much validity in this, and we join in the "hope that they [laymen] will lend their energetic assistance to every apostolic and missionary program of this, their ecclesial family."

The problem remains: Given the secular competence of the present-day layman, can it be presumed that the average parish has the competence to train him adequately in the apostolate? And even if the one, two, or three priests of the parish staff, together with ancillary personnel, did have this formative competence, is the parish the effective means of organizing today's apostolate?

MARVIN BORDELON

11.

On the family

*T*he conjugal and familial apostolate has special importance both for the Church and for civil society. For the Creator of all things established the conjugal partnership as the beginning and basis of human society and by his grace has made it a great sacrament in Christ and in the Church (see Eph. 5:32).

Christian couples are cooperators in grace and witnesses of faith to each other, their children, and other members of the household. To their children they give the first introduction and instruction in the faith; by word and example they form them for a Christian and apostolic life, counsel them wisely in selecting their own vocation, and carefully nourish a sacred vocation should they detect its presence.

It has always been the duty of married couples to give witness and proof by their lives to the indissolubility and sanctity of marriage, to insist vigorously on the right and obligation of parents and teachers to give their offspring a Christian education, and to uphold the dignity and lawful autonomy of the family. Today these constitute the most important part of their apostolate. They and other members of the faithful should work together with men of good will to see that these rights are upheld in civil legislation. They should see that in social planning there is due concern for family needs related to housing, education of children, working conditions, social security, and tax structures. Further the unity of the family should be carefully protected in arrangements for the movement of large groups of people.[4]

The family was established by God as the vital and fundamental cell of society. To fulfill its divine purpose it should, by the mutual devotion of its members and by their prayer made in common to God, become, as it were, a domestic extension of the Church's sanctuary; the whole family should involve itself in the liturgical worship of the Church; finally the family should show itself hospitable, just, and generous of its resources in the service of all its brethren who are in need. Among the various tasks of the family apostolate, these may be mentioned: the adoption of abandoned children, offering hospitality to the stranger, assistance in the operation of schools, counseling, and material assistance for adolescents, the preparation of engaged couples for marriage, catechetical work, support for couples and families involved in financial or moral difficulty, help to the aging by securing for them not only the necessities of life but also an equitable share in the profits of an expanding economy.

In every case the most treasured witness of Christ to the world is given by Christian families who cling to the Gospel and radiate an example of Christian marriage by their whole style of life.[5] This is especially true in lands where the seeds of the Gospel are just being sown, or where the Church is still in its infancy, or where it is racked by some critical difficulty.

The organization of families into certain kinds of associations can lend itself to the more effective achievement of the goals of this apostolate.[6]

Husbands, love your wives, just as Christ also loved the Church, and delivered himself up for her (Eph. 5:25).

COMMENT

Those engaged in the family apostolates must be pleased that their work has been mentioned in a chapter of a decree devoted to the laity, even though many of the ideas articulated are a reformulation of the tried-and-true.

What is surprising is that even some of the familiar ideas, the ideas that the Christian Family Movement has been talking about and acting upon for many years, are absent in this article on the family. A brief listing may illustrate the point:

The importance of happiness in marriage; the mystery of conjugal life and the value of conjugal love; the family as the ideal and ultimately the most important place for its members to learn to love God and the world; the breath-taking challenge and responsibility of parents—these have been talked about so often and at such great length in family apostolates as to have become platitudes.

If parents love one another and learn to love God and love the world, charity will become a valuable reality. If parents are humble, open-minded, meek and patient, as well as courageous, they will help to solve the problems of today and tomorrow.

Only those who are extraordinarily blessed will achieve these virtues quickly. For most of us, reaching them is a life-long objective. We must work; we must train ourselves. To learn, one must study; to act with conviction and purpose and understanding, one must train one's self. Systematic study and discussion that lead to quiet action within the world are characteristic of the approach that has produced positive values in the married apostolate.

MR. AND MRS. PATRICK CROWLEY

For the family apostolate to achieve its important goals of giving Christian guidance and education to children and active participation in bringing Christian principles into all areas of the world, the parish must provide the necessary spiritual formation and encouragement for such action. A critical difficulty lies in the absence of dialogue between the laity and parish clergy at this time. The past and present environment is and has been hostile for lay action. Parishes are child-centered, revolving around schools and their administration and financing, with little or no adult formation provided.

Vatican II urges the laity to avail themselves of all means of formation. But in many areas the local parish is the only potential source of education and formation (such as retreats, days of recollection, seminars, lectures, etc.). Such activities should be organized by the laity in cooperation and with the encouragement of the clergy. For then truly will the family become a "domestic extension of the Church's sanctuary."

We do not mean to say that the family apostolate must stay within the confines of the parish community. By the very nature of the family it must extend to all areas: work, community, politics, education, works of mercy, economics, etc. But in America we feel that a truly effective and vital family apostolate must begin with the local parish.

Unless parishes become family-centered and in particular adult-centered the family apostolate will never become a reality as an organized, effective force in American society.

MR. AND MRS. JOHN CIHI

What is an apostolic family? Certainly it is one that offers hospitality to strangers. Does this mean that a family must open its home to foreign students? In fact, it means more than that. It means that, in addition, there be an informal atmosphere of hospitality, one in which children are encouraged to bring home their playmates, out-of-town co-workers find relief from the dreariness of motel life, teen-agers feel free to gather and play records, and neither spouse hesitates to use the home for various group meetings, discussions, etc.

Such a family, too, might be noted for the fact that one of the spouses has expended an extra effort in establishing equal employment practices at his firm, or the adoption of open housing standards in the local community. Just the example of so dedicated a family is support of the highest order to a world deep in moral difficulty.

Just as the bishops spent four years working on this Decree (and others), so must couples everywhere take up the interpretation and discussion begun here. They must pray together. They must form within themselves a Christian attitude on issues affecting family life. Their children must reflect that Christian attitude. They must support the organization of families into associations dedicated to a more effective implementation of these teachings. When a family is all of these things, then that family will be an apostolic family.

MR. AND MRS. DONALD KRAFT

*I*n modern society young people exert a most significant influence.[7] Their life situation, mental outlook, and even their relationship to their own families, have considerably changed. Frequently their transition to a new social and economic status is too rapid. Moreover, while their social and even political impact steadily increases, they seem almost unequal to the task of adequately fulfilling these new responsibilities.

12.

On youth

The increased influence they wield in society requires of them a proportionate apostolic activity. And the natural endowments of youth equip them for such an apostolate. As the awareness of their own personality grows, their enthusiasm for life and their youthful energies make them want to take on their own responsibilities and become involved in social and cultural life. If this enthusiasm be touched with the spirit of Christ, and enlivened with an obedient love for the Church, it can produce very fruitful results. Young persons themselves, then, should become the first and immediate apostles to other youth, exercising an apostolate of their own among themselves, with some consideration for the social environment of the place where they live.[8]

Adults should carefully establish friendly channels of communication with young people which will allow both to overcome the chasm of age difference. They will then be able to understand each other and share with one another the insights which both possess. By example first, and, when occasion offers, by wise counsel and strong supportive assistance, adults should encourage young people to engage in the apostolate. On their part, young people should cultivate respect and trust toward adults and, granting their natural attraction for what is new, they should hold a proper esteem for the worthwhile traditions of the past.

Children too should have their own apostolic activities. According to their abilities, they also are true and living witnesses of Christ to their peers.

COMMENT

Adults seriously involved with young people in any kind of apostolate today must be prepared and willing to run certain risks. Not only is the work likely to be slow, painstaking, and most often without immediate results, but in some cases it may seemingly produce the very opposite effects hoped for. For young people to come to any profound awareness of what it means to be a Christian in this day often entails a crisis of faith —a period of search, rethinking, doubt, perhaps temporary alienation from the Church, disaffection with traditional norms of Christian morality and religious practice, and reaction against the institutional structures of the Church, including even the sacramental and hierarchical structures. The alienation may further extend to the family, to social and political structures, and other authoritarian structures in the young person's life as he struggles to achieve the "dignity and freedom of the Sons of God" as the Constitution on the Church, *Lumen Gentium,* puts it.

The paradox is that in the midst of these very crises, the young person himself may for the first time in his life be discovering and living an authentic Christian life, manifesting a deep Christian love for his fellow-men, particularly the underprivileged, by participation in all kinds of communitarian experiences, such as social protest movements, civil rights, Catholic Action, and student political movements.

Ought we to worry about these effects when we see them happen? I think not. We ought to be concerned, not as alarmists, but as friends, sympathetic listeners, with a deep faith ourselves in the youth we serve and a quiet confidence that all this is a sure sign that the Spirit is at work. Looking back on our own lives, I am sure most of us faced similar crises in our first discoveries of the demands of Christianity. At least, we should have.

VINCENT J. GIESE

The affluent young society of our time is properly cited in this article for what it is: a source of Christian energy in the apostolic work of the whole people of God. "Doing things" in a responsible and active way, is far more appealing to youth than "knowing things" about Christian life in a passive way. Surely children and young people in their teens can no longer be regarded as "future possible Christians." They are already involved in the call and response of faith, whatever the stage of their maturity.

Modern youth evidences a remarkable concern for involvement with others—for the poor, underprivileged, and needy. This is a response from a generation which never knew the Depression and knows hard times almost solely from vicarious experience. Witness the reception given by the young to the Peace Corps, PAVLA, civil rights, Operation Summertime, Operation Head-Start, and similar outlets for creative Christian apostolic work.

There are hopeful signs that the Christian message of loving service for others is "getting through." Possibly this is because of the emphasis in religious education today upon the importance of realizing what it is to be a Christian sharing God's life by grace. It is not unlikely either that the modern social apostolate recommends itself to Catholic youth in terms less reminiscent of the legionary, military, medieval, and pious-sounding "crusades" of another age.

WILLIAM J. REEDY

The temptations to steer young people down the paths we think best, to form their personalities to be images of our own, to impose upon them concerns that are ours and not theirs, to protect them from their own mistakes, to do their work for them when they fail to act responsibly, to make their decisions when they hesitate, to exploit their hero worship for our own needs—such temptations are strong indeed and, if the truth be told, have not always been overcome in "youth work" in the American Church. We have been all too reluctant to respect the freedom, the uniqueness, the independence of young people and hence we have often frightened away from our organizations the most talented and creative and have instead attracted the dependent and the mediocre, who have in the final analysis helped neither themselves nor their own generation nor the Church.

The Fathers of the Council indicate what we must do if we are to earn the respect and trust of young people. We must point out to them the variety of works to be done in the Church, make our resources available to them if they seek our help, encourage them when they encounter trials and difficulty, but always respect their integrity and freedom. Such an approach takes a great deal of faith—in both the goodness and zeal of the young person as well as the power of the Holy Spirit who we presume is inspiring them. Only when we are willing to love them and support them despite the mistakes which youthful enthusiasm and inexperience may cause, can we expect them to believe that we are sincere about wanting them to be free.

ANDREW GREELEY

13.
On the social environment

*B*y this apostolate is meant the effort to touch with the Christian spirit the attitudes, morals, laws, and community structures in which one lives. This apostolate is so much the province and function of lay people that it should scarcely ever be attempted by anyone else. In this area lay people can carry out the apostolate of "like to like." Here they complement the witness of their example by the witness of their speech.[9] Here they are the ones best able to assist their brothers, whether the apostolate be one related to work, professional or academic life, the neighborhood, recreation or community activities.

Lay people carry out this mission of the Church to the secular order first and foremost by that inner consistency of works with faith, by which they become the light of the world, and by a constant integrity of life which attracts others to love what is true and good, and eventually brings them to Christ and the Church. Equally important is that fraternal love which makes them share in the life, labors, sorrows, and aspirations of their fellow-men and thus gently but surely disposes their hearts for the workings of grace. They fulfill this mission finally by that mature awareness of their role in building up society which motivates them to carry out their domestic, social, and professional functions with such Christian generosity that their very manner of acting gradually penetrates the environment in which they live and work.

This apostolate should be extended toward all persons, no matter where they be encountered, and should include every spiritual and material benefit which can be offered. But true apostles will not be satisfied with this alone; they will seek to announce Christ to their neighbor by their words also. For many people will be able to hear the Gospel and acknowledge Christ only through the lay people who are close to them.

COMMENT

In the decree on the laity, the apostolic work of the Church is divided into four analytically distinct areas: 1) the spreading of the Gospel, 2) the sanctification of mankind, 3) the reconstruction of the social order, and 4) works of charity to the immediately suffering neighbor.

In the preaching of the Gospel and the sanctification of man, the clergy have priority in planning direction and setting up programs of action, and the laity are invited to help in this ministry of the Word and sacrament. In the works of charity to the suffering—the poor, the refugee, the ignorant, the ill, the retarded—a full-time living-commitment is called for. This suggests a primacy of emphasis for those in vows, since they can focus their compassion on others and their life on service despite the endless need. In the third area, however, the reconstruction of the social order, the work to which the world is now awakening, the mandate to lead is clearly given to the laity. In this area, he who is aware becomes responsible for the final product of all Christian effort—a new world.

Were the laity to take the mandate seriously, and clergy and religious as well, a working model for the true expression of love of God and neighbor would be operationalized in short order. There would be guidance from the Word, support from the sacraments, spiritual retreat for renewal, assurance of continued care for the suffering, and a mandate to experiment in the reconstruction of the social order.

SISTER MARIE AUGUSTA NEAL, S.N.D.

The Church teaches here what is known in the heart of every man: a dedicated life of integrity and love cannot fail to have an influence around itself. Our bishops and their priests have a most se-rious obligation to sensitize us to suffering and opportunity; and we have an obligation to work with them and listen to the Gospel, so that it is truly a witness to Christ which we give.

A weakness of the article lies in the fact that there is here no hint of an organized witness to produce social change, inspired by the Gospel. While responsibility is born by the individual, psychologists tell us that social groups and pressures may severely restrict one's freedom. On the other hand action taken in concert with others — social, political, etc. — is a profoundly sound way to help form a social environment which reflects the truth and love which is the message of our Lord.

Missing in the whole of chapter III, as well as in article 13, is a needed emphasis on the responsibility of lay Christians to exert their individual and collective responsibility to insure that the inevitable Church institutions which interact with secular ones, do so in an affirmative, leavening way. The magisterium would find it difficult, for example, to persuade employers who are Christians to pay a just wage to their employees, if Church employees themselves are not paid such a wage. So there is a dual responsibility in a Christianity so institutionalized: 1) to witness within the Christian community, at the invitation of the bishops and at times perhaps the Holy Spirit alone, and 2) to make a loving expression of Christian belief in individual and organized action in secular society.

MATHEW H. AHMANN

There is a great difference between this decree and the encyclical *Quadragesimo Anno* of 1930. The encyclical is not without the triumphalism so greatly deplored by Bishop de Smedt of Bruges during the Council, since it claimed in so many words the social betterment and enlightened legislation of society as an achievement of the encyclical.

In almost sixty years the Church has become more modest in its claims and acknowledges the still-prevailing irrelevance of Church documents during the gigantic combat of socialism and capitalism. The Church has learned to see differences better.

It becomes clear that this represents a drastically different view of the condition in which the Church lives. There is almost a visible withdrawal from the front-lines to the more profound action on the spirit. It is not the Church's task to erect an empire of goodwill and charity.

In a pluralistic society the working of the Church must be more subtle and also more indirect. What the Church now claims is that her lay apostles must be more humble and work from the outside into the center of the faith. The target of the Church's effort is the spirit, the mentality, customs, laws, and structures—not the objective conditions of society.

This wise retrenchment is the mark of honesty in the face of the apostolate of the laity. We have not even begun to understand this new attitude. It is on a much higher level and will have to say something definite when it measures its task now before itself.

The modesty of the claims is at first surprising, but becomes understandable when the futility of the old attitude is openly confessed. It seems that John XXIII and Paul VI have shown great courage and trust in the layman when they even propose closer cooperation with totalitarian states. The hands of competent laymen will be more blessed than those of the most gifted clerics.

H. A. REINHOLD

14.
The nation and the international order

*T*he nation and the international order constitute a vast area for the apostolate. Here lay people especially are the bearers of Christian wisdom. For motives of patriotism and the faithful execution of their civic duty, Catholics should feel themselves obliged to promote what is genuinely the common good. They should see that the weight of their opinion favors the just exercise of civil power and the conformity of civil law to the precepts of morality and the common good. Catholics with political abilities who are also, as they should be, strong in faith and in Christian understanding should not avoid public office, where by filling the office in a worthy manner they can at once work for the common good and prepare the way for the Gospel.

Catholics should welcome cooperation with all men of good will to encourage whatever is true, whatever is just, whatever is holy, whatever is lovable (see Phil. 4:8). They should meet with them, rival them in prudence and regard for mankind, and study how our social and public institutions can be improved according to the spirit of the Gospels.

Among the phenomena of our times worthy of special mention is the growing and inevitable sense of the solidarity of all peoples. Lay people in their apostolate should earnestly promote this sense of solidarity and transform it into a sincere and genuine fraternal love. Beyond this, lay people should be aware of international developments, and of the problems and solutions, both practical and theoretical, relating to this field, particularly those concerning the developing nations.[10]

All who work in or give assistance to foreign nations should bear in mind that relations between people should be a truly fraternal exchange, in which both giving and receiving is mutual. Lastly, let all who travel, whether for reasons of state, business, or pleasure, remember that wherever they go they are messengers of Christ and that they should conduct themselves as such.

Praise the Lord, all you nations; glorify him, all you peoples!
(Ps. 116:1).

COMMENT

The tone is set for article 14 in article 7, where it states flatly that "all that makes up the secular order . . . the economic order . . . political institutions . . . international relations . . . are not merely means to assist man toward his final goal. *They have a validity of their own."*

An appreciation of this simple but profound truth is the chief reason that the lay apostolate movement in the United States attained adulthood. How did it happen? Many factors would go into an explanation. Maritain's *True Humanism,* Guardini's *Spirit of the Liturgy,* Teilhard de Chardin's incarnational view of the world and the related trend in theology with the horrendous name of "desacralization"—all played a role in the development that has made the contemporary lay apostle a man of the world, a secular man. Only a decade or two ago, one had a picture of the "lay apostle" running out from his Catholic Action cell meeting to bring Christ to a secular if not evil world—rather like a member of a raiding party riding out from the safety of a pioneer fortress and then galloping back into his safe haven. What a different view of the world and the Christian's place in it is reflected in this Decree. "God saw that all he had made was very good" (Gen. 1:31).

But this new maturity, this appreciation of the proper value of the work of the world, places greater obligations on the new lay apostle. When he reads in article 14 that "lay people especially are the bearers of Christian wisdom," he knows that an individual Christian bears at best only a small parcel of that wisdom. And when he reads of his obligation "to promote what is genuinely the common good," he knows that the toughest problem for the citizen or the public official in this very complex world is to define the "common good" in particular circumstances. He also knows that to define the common good in, for example, an area as complex as economic development requires competence in his discipline that goes far beyond what in a more primitive age of the lay apostolate was called "the Catholic viewpoint."

The harmony becomes more apparent. What was naturally good, what had a validity of its own, what was worth studying in its own right, becomes in the final analysis the indispensable tool for a really effective lay apostle, one fully capable of playing his role in the Incarnation.

WILLIAM J. NAGLE

"The nation and the international order" condensed into one page! The Council Fathers evidently felt that it could not really be done. Still they tried their best to squeeze in all this "vast area." One world-embracing idea crowds on top of another in jostled, jumbled profusion.

But Pope John, thank God, gave us *Pacem in Terris,* which this article really seconds and ineptly summarizes. So back to that source, as well as to parts of *Mater et Magistra,* to really dig out the meaning for this area of the apostolate. Also, we can turn to Schema 13 of the Council, the Constitution on the Church in the Modern World.

This last-named Constitution, overall, takes a much more positive, progressive, even aggressive, stance than does the Decree on the Apostolate of the Laity—in large part because it takes enough space and words to come to grips with each sweeping subject. It stresses man's needs and achievement, human and social progress.

Whereas the laity decree timidly allows that Catholics "should not avoid public office," the modern-world constitution praises those who "devote themselves to the service of the state," and urges Christians to "fight for justice" and socio-economic development, as the way to the prosperity and peace of all mankind.

In short, the Constitution on the Church in the Modern World puts forth the "what" the laity deals with and handles on Monday morning. So the two Council documents must be mated to beget an apostolate for this world, here on earth today, especially in the apostolate's new world-wide dimension, in which Christian concern for national social justice matures into social justice among all the human family.

World justice, development and peace, promoted and governed by world law, enforceable by a world authority: this is the new dimension of the lay apostolate, so vast that the Decree stammered and stumbled in the rush to get it all out.

JOSEPH B. GREMILLION

IV

On various types of the apostolate

15.
Introduction

Lay people can exercise the apostolate either as individuals or in a variety of groups and associations.

16.
The importance and variety of the individual apostolate

The apostolate of the individual is a witness that springs up abundantly from the well-spring of a truly Christian life (see John 4:14). It is the source and condition on which all other apostolates, including those of organizations, are founded. Nothing else can be a substitute for it. Some lay people may lack the opportunity or ability to work together in apostolic associations. But all, whatever their situation, are invited and obliged to carry out the apostolate of the individual, which is in every instance a valuable apostolate, and in some situations the only one that can achieve results.

This apostolate has many forms by which lay people can build up the Church, sanctify the secular order and breathe the spirit of Christ into it.

One form of the individual apostolate is most appropriate for our times because it manifests Christ living in his believing followers. That is the witness of an entire lay life which is rooted in faith, hope, and charity. Beyond this, the apostolate of the spoken word, which in certain situations is the required one, enables lay people to announce Christ, to explain his teaching, to spread it in a measure fitted to each one's ability and circumstances, and to profess it faithfully.

Further, while they work together as citizens to maintain and extend the secular order, lay people should search for still higher motivations in the light of faith for the conduct of family, professional, cultural, and social affairs. Whenever the occasion offers they should make these motivations clear to others, conscious that by so doing they are cooperating with and offering praise to God the creator, redeemer, and sanctifier.

Finally lay people should quicken their lives with charity and, wherever they can, express that charity in works.

Let all remember that they can reach others and contribute to the redemption of the world by prayer and public worship, and by penance and the willing acceptance of life's toils and hardships, by which they are conformed to the suffering Christ (see 2 Cor. 4:10; Col. 1:24).

Now there are varieties of gifts, but the same Spirit;
and there are varieties of ministries, but the same Lord
(1 Cor. 12:4, 5).

COMMENT

The heart of the individual apostolate, according to article 16, lies in living a life which manifests Christ to the world. This manifestation takes place through a life rooted in faith, hope, charity, good works, a life of prayer, worship, and penance. There is nothing new in this observation.

The article does not indicate how the secular order is to be Christianized. The entire social apostolate is placed in the motives of Christians and in their efforts to bring people to Christ. Article 16 seems to ignore what is said in article 7: that the Christian must be interested in the temporal order because it has value in itself. We cannot quarrel with the fact that we must breathe a Christian spirit into the social order and through our activities bring people to Christ, but the document sounds as if we were to use the temporal order as a means of conversion rather than respect it for having value in itself because it is good and human and redeemed.

Article 16 explains this individual apostolate in terms of the least common denominator. Anyone who does not try to do what it outlines could hardly be called a practicing Christian. No mention is made of the truly dedicated individual who is willing to devote his life to overcoming injustice or to probing the secrets of nature in order to develop a world which more fully manifests that it has been redeemed, along with men.

Good will, charity, and penance, by themselves, will not produce a good Christian social order. The individual must be deeply concerned. He must understand the problems and inner laws of the temporal order and he must be truly competent in the work he does. Group action is impossible without this individual concern and responsibility. In a few words, article 16 does not go far enough in defining the individual's apostolate, and it does not reflect the experience of the Church in the last few decades with individual apostolic laymen.

GERARD P. WEBER

The article urges that lay people search for "higher motivations in the light of faith" and "make these motivations clear to others . . . that by so doing they are . . . offering praise to God." Does this imply that the motivation of extending the secular order and working for the good of the neighbor is a lesser motivation and does not praise God? If the world and man do not have a value in themselves, and if working in the world and responding to the needs of one's neighbor, just because he is a person, are not motivation enough, then what does the Incarnation mean? By and large, this article of the decree and a great part of the total work, speak in a language, and express a theology, which was more at home in the thirties and forties than it is in 1966.

LOUIS A. MARRONE

The heavy stress article 16 lays on the individual apostolate deserves thoughtful consideration: "It is the source and condition on which all other apostolates, including those of organizations, are founded. Nothing else can be a substitute for it."

All forms of organized apostolic work as well as individual effort will grow and increase to the extent that each and every Catholic is first imbued with a strong sense of mission and a personal responsibility to sanctify the secular order.

A Christian begins his life with baptism and draws nourishment from a meaningful community celebration of the Eucharist. But his growth remains stunted unless he reaches out to the wider community, as well as to the nation and the world.

If Council decrees are to be implemented by individuals and organizations, priests, religious teachers, and informed laymen will need to make strenuous efforts to develop the sense of apostolic responsibility that characterizes such persons as the following: 1) *the couple in Minnesota* who closed their new home to return to a difficult job with the government in Washington . . . 2) *the Hollywood scriptwriter* with 50 shows to his credit who has gotten ahead "without hiding, avoiding, bending or otherwise conceding my morality." . . . 3) *the bank manager in Connecticut* who extends fair credit terms to people in a run-down neighborhood where they had been burdened by high interest rates . . . 4) *the trade unionist in the West* who is doing his best to "restore integrity to business and labor relations and work for the dignity of man." . . . 5) *the college student in N. Y.* who switched his major to political science "to devote my life to better government and a better world."

JAMES KELLER

17.

The individual apostolate in some special circumstances

*T*he individual apostolate is urgently needed in areas where the Church's liberty of action is seriously curtailed. Under these difficult circumstances lay people take the place of their priests as far as possible, even at the risk of their own liberty and lives. They instruct those around them in Christian doctrine, encourage them to a religious life and Catholic outlook, and lead them to frequent reception of the sacraments and especially to cultivating a devotion to the Eucharist.[1] While heartily thanking God for continuing even in our day to inspire lay people to heroic courage in the midst of persecution, this holy synod with fatherly affection and grateful heart embraces these lay people.

The individual apostolate has particular significance in areas where Catholics are scattered and few in number. For the reasons cited or for special reasons arising from their professional occupations, some lay people work in the apostolate only as individuals. Such persons may well gather for serious interchanges in small groups without any more formal kind of organization, provided they always evidence to others, as a witness of their true charity, the clear indication that they are a community of the Church.

Unto this, indeed, you have been called, because Christ also has suffered for you, leaving you an example that you may follow in his steps (1 Pet. 2:21).

COMMENT

As the article points out, man is by nature social. He draws a large measure of his strength and wisdom from his association with others. When he is forced to work alone, he is quickly discouraged by adversity and easily led away from his original goals by expediency. Either of these dangers is fatal to the apostolate.

Yet, looking at the world as a whole, it is precisely under these circumstances that most lay people are called to exercise their apostolate. Even where the Church is established, these circumstances prevail. In the South and the Southwest in the United States, the number of Catholics is so small that individuals must largely work alone. In the most populated areas, the Church often is so comfortable and complacent that some individuals are forced by conscience to exercise an apostolate alone and even against that witness given by the clergy and members of their own Church.

The article goes on to say that such persons may well gather for serious interchanges in small groups without any more formal kind of organization. This is true, but it does not attack the most serious part of the problem. In fact, our schools and our parishes should provide the structure and challenge needed to support the lay apostolate. That these two institutions have largely failed to prepare lay people for their apostolate, or to orient them toward meaningful work in the social order is our greatest problem. No small groups for "serious interchanges" will make up for this lack. But, within a parish which was a real community filled with true Christian spirit, the individual apostle would find ample sources of courage and wisdom.

JAMES L. COCKRELL, JR.

With the spirit of true Christian love, an individual layman may find it necessary to teach, preach, and, through his Christian witness, sanctify those members charged to him by Christ. Although in this country the layman is not hindered by government in the exercise of his right to worship, teach, or witness to his Christian commitment, circumstances sometimes call for the practice of heroic virtue in certain apostolic undertakings. By affirmatively answering the call of Christ and cooperating with the grace of God, the sanctification of the layman is assured as well as the strengthening of the whole Mystical Body. Because the individual layman in the world may find himself alone in the crowd, it is important that he join in serious discussion with others like himself, so that in the spirit of Christian charity this group may carry on a dialogue which gives witness to the fact that it is a charismatic community of the Church.

JAMES BELANGER

It can be seriously questioned in reference to this article, whether *any* Christian should habitually act only as an individual, alone. What has become here of the conciliar insight that there are people of God in vast numbers outside the ecclesial community of Roman Catholicism, that Christian apostolic action is far more extensive than the organized, public efforts of the Church? The Constitution on the Church affirmed that the Christian always has a specifically Christian and lay apostolate in the very heart of *all* secular concerns, therein to join *with all his human brothers.*

The difficulty in this article stems, in fact, from a return to a distinction in the layman's role abandoned in the more basic Constitution on the Church: the distinction between "within the Church" and "in the secular order." The Constitution states that the laity's vocation *within the Church* is to the temporal order (ch. 4, art. 31). The laity are never driven to "take the place of their priests" to find a superabundance of Christian work to do.

JOHN J. RYAN

18.
The importance of organizations

*A*ll the Christian faithful as individuals are summoned to exercise the apostolate in the various situations of their lives. Yet we must remember that by his nature man is a social being. It has pleased God to gather those who believe in Christ into the people of God (1 Pet. 2:5,10) and unite them in one body (see 1 Cor. 12:12). The organized apostolate of the faithful thus happily answers both a human and a Christian need. At the same time it symbolizes the unity and community of the Church in Christ, who said: "Wherever two or three are assembled in my name, there I am in the midst of them" (Matt. 18:20).

For that reason the faithful should exercise their apostolate by uniting their efforts with one another.[2] They should be apostles in the community of the home, in their parishes and dioceses, which themselves express the community character of the apostolate, and in freely chosen societies which they decide to form among themselves.

Another reason for the importance of the organized apostolate is that, both in church communities and in various secular environments, the apostolate can only be effective through the concerted action of many. The organizations established to provide concerted action in the apostolate act as a support for their members, form them for the apostolate, organize and supervise their apostolic work. More effective results can thus be expected than if each one were acting independently.

In our present situation, as far as the work of lay people is concerned, we very much need to strengthen the organized and federative form of the apostolate. Only the close coordination of our resources will enable us to protect apostolic values adequately and achieve all the goals of the modern apostolate.[3] Here it is particularly important to note that the apostolate should reach out to the ordinary mentality and social situation of those to whom it is directed. Otherwise they will often falter under the pressure of public opinion or of other institutions in society.

But as it is, God has set the members, each of them, in the body as he willed . . . Now you are the body of Christ, member for member (1 Cor. 12:18, 27).

COMMENT

Whether we like it or not, we are social creatures, greatly influenced by our environment and by the views of those with whom we live. Occasionally the world sees a charismatic figure, such as Pope John XXIII or Winston Churchill, who by superior insights can influence an entire generation. But such charisms are rare. Most of us achieve results through our collective influence upon a community, neighborhood, or place of work.

A good example of the power of successful organization was the passage of the Civil Rights Act of 1964. Practical politicians felt for a long time that it would be impossible to get congressional assent for so strong a piece of legislation. But when churches and synagogues, civil-rights and minority groups, labor organizations, and the like, spoke as one, our legislators listened.

Looking forward to the future, the crucial problems of the inner city, and the correlative problem of open occupancy in all housing, are challenges which call for both organization and persistence. Issues must be studied. We must look for successful programs to serve as models. We must seek allies everywhere. Then we must act.

Many problems beset us in our communities today. If we restrict our reaction to discussion, deploring, and passing resolutions, our influence will be minimal. From the Church we can get moral guidance and inspiration. But then we must march out, arm-in-arm with men of all religions and even men who have good will but no religious faith, and make the world truly human, so that God can then remake men in his image.

JOHN F. CRONIN, S.S.

There is no special apostolate of the laity; there are specialized tasks within the one apostolate of the Mystical Body of Christ. We all—hierarchy, religious, laity—share the same apostolate.

Again, though we may treat of an individual apostolate and an organized apostolate, there are not two separate apostolates. A Christian doing an individual action is joined in the community of all Christians doing other individual actions and carrying out social or organized actions.

This section on the importance of organizations is sorely needed in the United States, where the rugged individualism in our social, economic, and cultural life is matched by similiar patterns in our worship and apostolate.

But as with the chicken-or-the-egg-first argument, it is practically impossible to determine whether the Jesus-and-me attitude in religious education and the liturgy came before "look out for number one" in the economic order.

I suspect that rugged individualism grew from the interaction between bad theology (e.g., excessive emphasis on indulgences) and a failure of Christians to see the spiritually progressive potential in the growth of humanism. Sharing the optimism of Teilhard de Chardin, I would give an edge to Christianity as being more affected by, than initiating this regressive trend of egocentrism.

I think that those who serve the apostolate through organized efforts have, as de Chardin describes it, "that great hope held in common." They are working for the Mystical Body of Christ through man's progress so that we may truly build the "City of God"—a community of persons.

BERNARD LYONS

I think article 18 is outdated and thus points us in the wrong direction. It is a statement of what is, rather than what should be. In a society that maintained more or less a union of Church and state, Church apostolic organizations served a purpose. As we move more and more into a secular society, I see little need for the organized lay apostolate, whether this be C.F.M., Catholic Interracial Councils, Catholic Charities, Legion of Mary, N.C.C.M., or any other. In a society with a clear distinction between the ecclesiastical and secular establishments, we need to do two things apostolically. One is to develop the Christian as an apostolic person in society. The other is to join hands with others of good will in secular groups to serve man. For example, in our town we made an extensive survey of the human situation only to find that for every major problem there was some political or secular organization concerned with it. Our Christians needed only to get involved in the organizations already established.

To strengthen apostolic organizations which are formative in purpose is to set up, in reality, substitute parishes. To strengthen other organizations with special missions, e.g. Catholic Interracial Councils, smacks of flying our own flag rather than humbly serving with others in a pluralistic effort. Besides, we will better solve the problems with others than by ourselves. The maintenance of our own unnecessary apostolic organizations also drains us of our energy and tempts us to become more concerned with institutions than with man himself.

WILLIAM NERIN

19.

On the wide variety of structure in the organized apostolate

*T*here is great variety among apostolic organizations.[4] Some have as their purpose the general apostolic goals of the Church; others specifically direct their efforts to sanctification and evangelization; still others work for the Christian enrichment of the secular order; some give their witness of Christ specifically through the works of charity and mercy.

Among these organizations we should prize highly those which advocate and foster a more intimate relationship between the faith of their members and their everyday lives. Organizations are not an end in themselves; they are rather instruments for service to the Church's mission in the world. Their apostolic value is rooted in the Christian witness and evangelical spirit of the whole organization, as well as the measure in which its goals coincide with the goals of the Church.

Looking both at the proliferation of institutions and the rapid pace of modern society, the universality of the Church's mission demands that the apostolic undertakings of Catholics should more and more be brought together in coordinating structures at the international level. International Catholic organizations will more readily achieve their goals when the organizations which unite to comprise them, and their memberships, are more closely related to the international entity itself.

Lay people have a right to form organizations, manage them,[5] and join them, provided they maintain the proper relationship to ecclesiastic authority.[6] However, they should beware of spreading their resources too thinly, and that is what happens when new organizations and operations are needlessly brought into existence. We also waste our resources when we keep in existence organizations and ways of doing things which are obsolete. Nor is it always best to transfer indiscriminately to other countries, the structures established in one place.[7]

COMMENT

What is granted to laymen in this article is the right to give organizations and societies the *form* laymen consider suitable to produce results.

Some might argue that the proviso concerning the need to "maintain a proper relationship to ecclesiastical authority" takes away with the left hand what the right has already given. But if lay and hierarchical functions are viewed as complementary, not involving the same functions in the Church, this should not be so. Without the proviso, the activity of the Church would be incomplete (witness without the word, for example).

Since lay people will be creating and changing structures in the Church, we must become more keenly aware of the kinds of structures in which the Christian spirit more easily comes alive. The Council has addressed the question negatively, giving cautions concerning dissipation of resources, continuance of inadequate tactics, retention of tired organizations, and selection of structures from other locales simply because they work *there*.

What the Council did not speak about, a field wide open for positive thought, experimentation, and reflection is: What kind of structures make for the best Christian witness, and most perfectly make faith, hope, and love present in a particular environment? For example, when do small groups and intermediate groupings produce better results than mass groupings? What structures make for freedom of action?

From the American lay apostolate experience, some tentative answers to such questions may be sought out and shared, one being that the relationship between structure and spirit is very intimate. Good structures allow for each man or woman to be treated as a person, permit give and take, consent, choice, and self-determination. Good structures allow for mutual exchange, even of ourselves. Good structures allow a timely and efficient accomplishment of the group purpose. If structures you know do not allow for these things, or do so only in small part, are they not ready for reform?

We have to approach structure tentatively, because in some degree even what we choose next will soon be ready for reform. Structure is really the servant of the Spirit that is in us.

PETER FOOTE

The paradox of this article, and of the Decree as a whole, is that it involves the official, institutional Church in the endorsement of what grew up in the face of, at best, general indifference from the institutional Church and, at worst, outright hostility from it. What gives the Decree its meaning and whatever strength it has is its recognition of the validity of the insights, aims, and methods, not of "Catholic Action," but of the specialized apostolic movements such as YCM (formerly YCW), YCS, and CFM. Those who fought, and that is the right word to use, to establish these movements will appreciate the irony of official recognition coming now. Still, to have the hierarchy acknowledge not only that lay people have the right to form their own apostolic organizations, which can accomplish good, but also to imply that this work is a concern of the whole Church, hierarchical and lay ("*We also waste our resources . . .*"), is a truly remarkable, perhaps even revolutionary, development.

Those who fought to bring about this revolution will know, however, that it is in no danger of being institutionalized; they will realize that the mild and sometimes ambiguous endorsement given to apostolic movements and their work in the Decree constitutes more an acknowledgment of good accomplished than a wholehearted mandate for lay initiative and independence in the future. They will know that the revolution is far from accomplished and that they must continue to work for it in exactly the same manner as before: with love for the Church, with respect for all in it, and with full awareness of how it operates as a human institution.

JOHN McCUDDEN

20.

Catholic Action

*T*he lay people of numerous countries, out of increasing zeal for the apostolate, have organized themselves over many decades into a variety of associations and action groups which, while pursuing directly apostolic goals, also maintain a rather close relation to the hierarchy. Among these and similar institutions, those known as "Catholic Action" are worthy of special recognition. They have commonly been described as "the cooperation of lay people in the apostolate of the hierarchy."[8] Deservedly, they have been recommended and promoted by the popes and numerous bishops, and they have achieved excellent results for the kingdom of Christ.

These forms of the apostolate, whether under the title "Catholic Action" or some other, have an important value for our times. They are characterized by the following combination of values:

a) The immediate goal of these organizations is the apostolic goal of the Church, that is, the evangelization and sanctification of men, and the formation in them of a Christian conscience, so that the spirit of the Gospel will be brought through them to their own environment and community.

b) While working with the hierarchy in the established way, lay people contribute their own experience and take responsibility for directing the organizations, determining the circumstances in which the pastoral action of the Church is to be exerted, and designing and executing the plan of action.

c) There is an organic unity to this kind of lay action, which makes their apostolate more effective and more pointedly portrays the community nature of the Church.

d) Whether acting on their own initiative or at the invitation of the hierarchy to cooperate in their apostolate, these lay people are ultimately under the guidance of the hierarchy itself. The hierarchy may also expressly approve this type of cooperation by mandate.

Organizations which in the hierarchy's judgment exhibit this combination of characteristics are to be recognized as Catholic Action, no matter what structures or titles they may have in various countries.

This holy council strongly recommends these organizations, which certainly answer the needs of the Church's apostolate in many lands. It invites priests and lay people working in them to seek an increasing verification in their groups of the characteristics outlined above, and commends to them a constant and brotherly cooperation with all other forms of the apostolate.

COMMENT

The immediate subject of this article is clearly the "formation" movements (e.g., YCS, YCM, CFM), as is apparent from the concluding clause of characteristic (a). There is a rather elusive ambivalence between the "formation" theme of characteristic (a) and the "action" theme of characteristic (b), which is a large part of the history of the movements themselves.

However, the article lays special stress on the proprietary interest of the hierarchy in this form of the apostolate. This stress, and the language of the first half of characteristic (a), when compared with articles 2, 6, and 7, show an intention to situate this form of the apostolate as one of "evangelizing and sanctifying," and thus "entrusted in a special way to the clergy" (art. 6), rather than as one of the "renewal of the secular order," which is the layman's "own proper task" (art. 7).

It is a special irony that the "participation" definition—the historic workhorse for all lay apostles—should now be reserved to a form so intimately connected with the particular apostolate of the hierarchy.

The main theme of this article seems to be the link between the call to "seek an increasing verification" and the broad charter of responsibility in characteristic (b). The Council clearly recognizes that the formation movements have outgrown the benevolent and saintly autocrats who gave them life. The movements now require constructive and open self-criticism and genuine, though obedient, self-determination. This will not be achieved without courage, charity, and humility in appropriate measure to the principal actors.

MICHAEL SCHILTZ

The phrase "cooperation of lay people in the apostolate of the hierarchy" suggests that the layman is an obedient subordinate and the bishop a sure, wise, superior guide. Would it not be better if this pre-conciliar phrase were exchanged for one which expressed the fresh and respectful spirit of Vatican II? The Constitution on the Church says that the laity in their own way are sharers in the priestly, prophetical, and kingly functions of Christ (art. 31). Why not say, "Lay people and bishops are associates in the work of Christ"? Or "Bishops and lay people are co-workers in the Church's apostolate"? For the whole Church, not just the hierarchy, receives Christ's command to bring the Gospel to all men.

Paragraph b has significance for members of the lay apostolate who feel the repressive grip of an overbearing chaplain. A serious obstacle to the progress of the lay apostolate has been the well-intentioned but unyielding chaplain who thinks the layman's purpose is to do the bidding of priests. If a group is not free to determine the circumstances under which it operates, it is not a Catholic Action group. Paragraph b is the layman's Magna Carta.

JOHN J. HILL

21.

On the appreciation of organizations

22.

Lay persons serving the Church in special groups

*A*ll apostolic organizations are to be properly appreciated. Those which the hierarchy has at various times and places praised or recommended, or whose establishment they have decreed to be more needed, should all be very highly esteemed by priests, religious, and lay people, and they should promote them to the extent of their abilities. Among them, international organizations and associations of Catholics are of particular importance today.

*W*orthy of special commendation and honor are those single and married lay persons who, either permanently or for a period of time, contribute their professional talents to Church institutions and their programs. We are equally pleased by the growing number of lay people who offer their assistance to apostolic organizations and programs at home, in the international field, and in Catholic missionary communities and newly established Churches.

The pastors of the Church should gladly and gratefully welcome these lay people. They should see that treatment of them is fully in keeping with the demands of justice, equity, and charity, with special attention to proper support for them and their families. They should also enjoy all necessary instruction, spiritual assistance, and incentive.

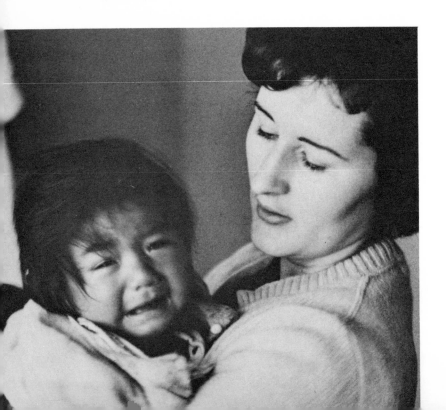

And if one member suffers anything, all the members suffer with it, or if one member glories, all the members rejoice with it (1 Cor. 12:26).

COMMENT

In addition to the diversity in the lay apostolate mentioned in preceding articles, there is a growing group of lay people who are working *full-time* in apostolic programs or organizations. In the United States, YCS and YCM have had such full-time (but temporary) workers developing their movements for years. Now, Papal and Extension Volunteers contribute full-time (but also temporary) service to the missions. But also, an increasing number of laymen are choosing such commitments on a long-term or permanent basis.

But laymen in such full-time work face a number of serious problems: primarily misunderstanding of their role in the Church and financial difficulties. The former difficulty is felt particularly by single persons who have chosen to work permanently in apostolic programs. They have often been regarded as no longer "lay" despite their style of life— not withdrawn *from,* but *in,* the world, and their wholehearted commitment of time and energies to develop the role of the layman in the Church and the world.

Article 22 has happily clarified their role by placing them clearly within the apostolate of the laity. Neither the choice of celibacy nor full-time work in apostolic programs removes one from the "laity." Although such verbal distinctions and clarifications may seem unimportant, they often have practical results in the acceptance of the contribution of those concerned.

Married couples, particularly, working full-time in the apostolate have suffered financial difficulties. It is obvious that many laymen are prevented from making a contribution in the lay movements solely because they cannot adequately support their families. Others continue their contribution, but at the cost of great financial sacrifice. The gentle suggestions in article 22 that such persons are worthy of special commendation and honor and that attention should be given by pastors to the proper financial support for them and their families are very happy inclusions. If followed, such practical remarks in the Decree on the Laity may do more to promote the apostolate than many generalizations.

VIRGINIA LEARY

Among our married laymen, but especially among those who are called to the single state, there is a potential which is virtually untapped. One area of immediate urgency for the use of such laymen is as lay catechists in the Confraternity of Christian Doctrine program. Besides the necessity of continuous instruction, spiritual assistance, and incentive for lay catechists, there should be the exploration of the possibility and perhaps necessity, in maintaining lay catechists of high caliber, of providing part-time pay for them.

Another area which needs imagination and study is the present status and goals of local parish organizations. Not only are they to be a service to the local parish, but also, as stated in chapter IV of the Constitution on the Church: "Now, the laity are called in a special way to make the Church present and operative in those places and circumstances where only through them can it become the salt of the earth." Preparing an enriched format for parish organizations, which would point not only to the needs of the local parish but also to the needs of the modern world, could profitably be begun at the grass-root levels by a full dialogue between pastor and parishioner.

H. J. MAJERUS

Professional men and women have received an abundance from God which they have cultivated in such a way as to give them a unique and recognized place in human society. As time clouds the memory of the American Catholic's immigrant origins, Catholics, in increasing numbers, have entered the ranks of the professions—all professions. The phenomenon of suburbia has juxtaposed these new Catholic professional men and women in numbers which, a few years ago, would have seemed fantastic. The time has come when the right order of things demands "new organs erected by the Church" (The Constitution on the Church) through which the Catholic professional man and woman can "share in the life, labors, sorrows, and aspirations" of those who, in one way or another, live in poverty.

Every parish with a sufficient number of professional people, be they doctors, lawyers, accountants, agronomists or what-not, could well establish a *professional clinic.* The clinic would bring all apostolic-minded professional people of the parish together into a pool. A place and scheduled hours could be provided and publicized by the parish administration which would put professional men and women in contact with people who need professional help and cannot afford it. Such apostolic action, started at the parish level, in many cases would naturally reach beyond the parish into the wider diocese and beyond the diocese into more distant needy areas at home and abroad.

Humanity needs the professional skills of Catholics given freely and out of love. Bishops, pastors and leaders of the apostolate of the laity need to set up instrumentalities to make this possible.

JOSIAH G. CHATHAM

V
Maintaining proper relations

23.

Introduction

*T*he apostolate of lay people, whether individual or in organizations, should be properly coordinated and fitted into the apostolate of the whole Church. In fact, an essential element of the Christian apostolate is its coordination under those designated by the Holy Spirit to rule the Church of God (see Acts 20:28). Equally necessary is cooperation between various undertakings of the apostolate, which likewise should be coordinated by the hierarchy.

A mutual appreciation for all forms of the apostolate, and a coordination of them that leaves intact the particular qualities of each,[1] is needed to secure a spirit of unity, so that destructive rivalries may be avoided, common goals achieved, and a spirit of fraternal charity radiated by the whole apostolate. And this is certainly most appropriate in a Church the nature of whose mission requires apostolic harmony and cooperation among clergy, religious, and lay people.

COMMENT

Vatican Council II was in great measure an exercise in communication (or dialogue) among the bishops. During nearly a year of almost daily sessions, the bishops progressed in their awareness and appreciation of that community of apostolic authority and responsibility which binds them together. The unique universal authority of our Holy Father was ever before them, always respected by them, and noticeably strengthened by his personal presence and attention. The recognition of collegiality, a community quality, was one precious fruit of this kind of communication. Without communication, the rediscovery of collegiality would have been most improbable.

The whole apostolate must be resplendent with "fraternal charity," mutual esteem, and "due respect." I venture to say that such desired qualities can be assured only through perseverance in communication and dialogue at all levels of authority, knowledge, and grace in the Church. What was accomplished among the bishops must in some suitable manner be repeated among the clergy, the religious, and the laity, as well as between these groups.

Particularly in the case of the laity must those in ecclesiastical authority learn to listen with attention and forbearance. May the fruitful growth of the lay apostolate not be jeopardized by the silent violence of presenting closed ears and minds to honest communication.

BISHOP VICTOR J. REED

In the early forties, when the specialized movements of the lay apostolate were in the first stages of their growth, there was much discussion as to what was Catholic Action and which organizations could lay claim to the title. There was even argument and rivalry between older, more traditional organizations and the new ones. Such rivalry hardly served the cause of the various organizations or the cause of the apostolate itself. This is the main point of this introductory paragraph for chapter V. Unity and charity are necessary for all the forms of the apostolate, not merely because these are required for efficient and effective work, but even more importantly because if these essentially Christian qualities are lacking Christ is not there.

One essential way of insuring unity in the lay apostolate is to center it about the bishop. He is the chief priest and shepherd of the diocese and it must be he who gives inspiration, direction, and coordination to the lay apostolate. The word "rule" used here in quotation from the Acts of the Apostles must be understood in the sense in which it is used in the Gospels and in the Constitution on the Church. As chief priest and shepherd, the bishop serves the people of God, and one of the ways in which he serves them is by helping them exercise their right and duty of taking part in the apostolate of the Church which is theirs by baptism.

JAMES J. KILLGALLON

*T*he hierarchy should promote the apostolate of lay people, provide the principles and spiritual aids, direct its use to the Church's common good, and see that doctrine and due order are preserved.

The apostolate of lay people has many purposes and structures, and it may have many kinds of relation to the hierarchy.

24.

Relations to the hierarchy

There are in the Church numerous apostolic programs undertaken at the free choice of lay people and wisely managed by them. In certain circumstances the Church's mission is better implemented by such programs, and thus the hierarchy frequently recommends and praises them.[2] However, no undertaking should claim the word "Catholic" for its title without the permission of legitimate ecclesiastical authority. Some forms of the apostolate are expressly recognized by the hierarchy, and in a variety of ways.

Further, to satisfy what the common good of the Church requires, the ecclesiastical authority may select and promote in a special way one or other of the apostolic organizations or programs which have a directly spiritual purpose. In such cases the hierarchy assumes a special responsibility. By thus directing the apostolate in various ways, as the situation dictates, the hierarchy associates some of its structures more closely with its own apostolic function. However, the proper nature and character of the two should be maintained, and lay people should retain the freedom to act on their own initiative. The hierarchical action referred to here is in many ecclesiastical documents called a "mandate."

Finally, the hierarchy entrusts to lay people some tasks which are more properly the duty of pastors, such as teaching Christian doctrine, certain liturgical ceremonies, and the care of souls. By virtue of such a commission, lay people fulfilling these functions are entirely subject to higher ecclesiastical direction.

Regarding institutions and programs directed to the secular order, the duty of the Church's hierarchy is to teach and provide an authentic explanation of the moral principles to be applied in the secular order. They also have the right, after enlisting the help of experts and weighing the matter carefully, to make judgments on whether such programs and institutions conform to moral principles, and to decide what is required to protect and promote supernatural values.

I, therefore, the prisoner in the Lord, exhort you to walk in a manner worthy of the calling with which you were called . . . careful to preserve the unity of the Spirit in the bond of peace (Eph. 4:1, 3).

COMMENT

Although it is only indirectly stressed in article 24 as in the entire decree, it nevertheless remains fairly clear that the apostolate of the layman is not merely the exercise of the hierarchy's commission, is not merely the organized public task of extending the ecclesiastical order as such. The "apostolate" of the layman is a considerably more informal thing than this, a thing only rarely recognizable in terms of organizations, groups, cells, etc. Since Christianity is not something appliqué, but rather is an ethos, the apostolate of the layman must be envisioned primarily as the spontaneous radiation of that ethos and not as the execution of some explicit episcopal directive or the pursuit of some structured program.

If secular history is salvation history when judged in the light of the Incarnation, then the above assertion is the religious rationale for the empirically verifiable fact that the layman, and more particularly the educated layman, wants as little as possible to do with the established organizations of the official apostolate. Nor by that fact does he see himself as any the less apostolic. In this sense he does not think of himself as being "sent," as "bearing" witness, as "bringing" Christ into the marketplace, the lecture hall, etc.; he finds himself in the marketplace, in the lecture hall or whatever, not by reason of any extrinsic impulse or motive, however "religious," but because of his natural inclination and disposition toward them; and it is by the unreflective—though by no means unintellectual—acceptance of this disposition that he effectively communicates what he is. He *is* a sign, he does not make himself one.

A similar kind of introspective scrupulosity which hesitates before the spontaneously organic is evident in the admonition in this article against the easy ascription of "the word 'Catholic'" to allegedly unauthorized activities. "Catholic" here seems to be conceived as a brand-name copyright by bishops and transferable only to approved licensees. Since "Catholic" is a title that can only mean, and can only be lived as meaning, "communion with the totality of things," one must hope that this recurring fear that every priest or layman acting in the secular sphere will be immediately identified by outsiders with the deposit of faith, with all creeds and councils and popes, etc., — one must hope that this fear will be recognized as groundless. One of the minor drawbacks of ecumenism seen as "movement" is that it has so intensified our confessional self-consciousness, has so heightened our respect for churchly labels that "Catholic" means other than "Christian," and "Christian" means other than "human"—the result being that we presumably can have Catholics and Christians lacking humanity.

JUSTUS GEORGE LAWLER

The structure of this article on the relations of the hierarchy and lay people is, in itself, interesting. It is didactic, as befits a decree, but it deals with a problem of lay polity according to an inverted approach. The issues of lay responsibility are looked at in relationship to the ecclesiastical structure. But the relations of lay people with bishops and everybody else must derive from the appropriate lay responses to the problems of our time in a world trembling with revolution. A major characteristic of the apostolate is that it is now individualized, vastly varied, and struggling in a tempestuous secular order and disorder that has its own laws and dynamics. Another characteristic is that it is classically weak in strategic social ideology and organizational forms. It is, therefore, a largely experimental and developmental phenomenon. The apostolate does not fit into the neat categories of the Decree. Its diversity and religious promise are its chief social resources at this time. The Decree is not shaped by these conditions of the apostolate. It is not world-centered, but is centered in a circumscribed ecclesiastical view.

The Decree lacks the clarion quality and the perspective of boldness, flexibility, and social insight that are required to stimulate the inventiveness needed to rescue the apostolate from the worn and mechanical categories in which it is fixed. There is too much of the past and too little of the present and the future in the document.

DENNIS CLARK

25.

On the support to be given to the apostolate of lay people by the clergy

*B*ishops, pastors, and priests, both diocesan and religious, should keep in mind that the right and duty of exercising the apostolate is shared by all the faithful, both lay and cleric. They should remember that lay people also have their own proper role in building up the Church.[3] Therefore as brothers they should work with lay people in the Church and for the Church, and show a special solicitude for lay people in their apostolic works.[4]

Priests who assist the special forms of the lay apostolate should be naturally endowed for the work, carefully selected, and suitably trained.[5] Those who are assigned to this ministry represent the hierarchy in their pastoral activities by reason of their appointment; they should be constantly faithful to the spirit and teaching of the Church and encourage desirable relationships between hierarchy and lay people; they should devote themselves to nourishing the spiritual life and apostolic motivation of the Catholic organizations entrusted to them; they should assist the apostolic activities of such groups with wise advice and encourage what they initiate. By a continuing dialogue with lay people they should carefully find out what structures make for a more productive apostolic effort; they should encourage a spirit of unity both within the organization and with other groups.

Finally religious nuns and brothers should respect the apostolic works of lay people, and willingly lend themselves to promote their programs, in keeping with the statutes and spirit of their own institutes;[6] and they should seek to complement, support and assist the function of priests in this work.

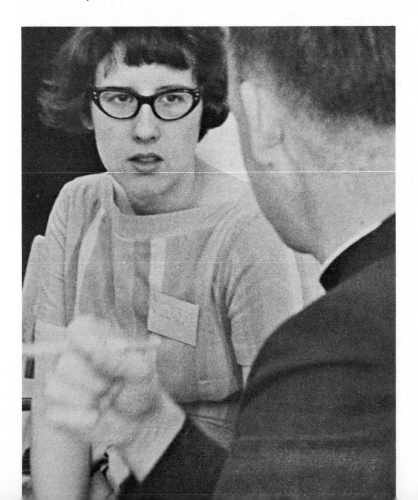

And whoever wishes to be first among you shall be the slave of all; for the Son of Man also has not come to be served but to serve, and to give his life as a ransom for many (Mark 10:44, 45).

COMMENT

In defining the nature of the Church, the Second Vatican Council has given us a new concept of the laity. Most of us have grown up with the notion of the laity as given by Pope Pius XI: that they can cooperate in the apostolate of the hierarchy—with the bishop's mandate. Now we are aware that the laity has a proper role in the apostolate. As bishops and priests, we must make the sometimes difficult step from the knowledge of what the Council tells us on this point to the realization of this truth in actual practice.

Before we are priests or bishops, we are lay people. We have not left the people of God because of our new position. We remain in the midst of our people as those who serve. We feed our people with the Word of God; we feed them with the Bread of Life. We guide them. In all these functions, we are called upon to serve "in the midst of the people," not apart from them.

We must have an increasing awareness that the Holy Spirit speaks not only through us but also through our people. We must ever be ready to listen.

Two convictions must dominate us as we serve our people:

1) There is a complete and mutual interdependence between priest and people. If our people need us, we certainly need our people—for the building up of the Body of Christ.

2) There must be a mutual spirit of trust between ourselves and our flocks. It is only by trusting each other that the freedom of all of God's holy people will be manifest and that the Holy Spirit will form us more perfectly as witnesses to the world of the death and resurrection of the Lord.

BISHOP CHARLES A. BUSWELL

Religious themselves, in order to help the laity in their apostolate, must inquire, discuss, evaluate, and adjust. They must cherish the essential, discard the irrelevant, and bravely chart new courses in obedience to the voice of the Church calling for this often painful effort. The norm of all change and training will be the mind of Christ as applied to the needs of the Church today. These needs can be met in a spirit of honest acceptance of what the times have to say to us. For the times speak with the voice of the Spirit urging us to meet needs by solutions which will be ecclesial, apostolic, and eminently social, since we must become increasingly conscious of our oneness with all men in God's people.

In addition to the apostolic schools they conduct, religious will help the pastor to re-educate his flock. They can give courses in the decrees themselves either in their own colleges in the evening, or in the parish itself. They might set up parish-level training schools, study sessions, discussion groups and meetings of the specialized movements such as CFM or YCS.

Complete mobilization of religious and priestly personnel requires retraining for those who have already completed the seminary or novitiate period. This can be given through the methods mentioned above, but, especially through summer sessions conducted by the diocese or at the religious community colleges. Even better would be the attendance of such personnel at the apostolic schools for laity, priests, and religious alike. This adaptation and retraining is absolutely necessary in the light of the work of Vatican II. It must be accepted

realistically in the same spirit in which our lay counterparts accept and embrace retraining (scientific, technical, administrative) as part of the price of survival in the modern professional world. Religious do not exist outside the temporal order. The modern Church has now begun to catch up with the pace of the modern world. Loyalty to Christ and his Church demands our prayerful, trusting efforts to step out with that Church upon the troubled waters of this world.

SISTER GERTRUDE JOSEPH
DONNELLY, C.S.J.

26.

On means for securing mutual cooperation

Wherever it is possible there should be diocesan councils which, through the cooperation of clergy and religious with lay people, can assist the apostolic work of the Church both in evangelizing and sanctifying, and in charitable, social, and other endeavors. Such councils will be helpful to the mutual coordination of various lay enterprises and organizations without threatening the autonomy and special character of each group.[7]

Such councils should also be established, as far as possible, in the parish, and on the inter-parish, inter-diocesan, national, and international levels.[8]

There should also be established at the Holy See some special secretariat to promote and serve the apostolate of lay people. It should be a center for facilitating communications relating to the various apostolic programs of lay people, for research on modern problems in this field, and for consultation that will help both hierarchy and lay people in their apostolic works.

The apostles and the presbyters had a meeting . . .
With the whole church [they] decided to select
representatives and to send them to Antioch with
Paul and Barnabas (Acts 15:6, 22).

COMMENT

The councils called for here can be a practical means of advancing the rejuvenation of the Church. The word "can" was used deliberately, because the success of the councils is not automatic. In fact, unless careful preparation is given both clergy and laity, the councils will cause more friction than good and we will have trusteeism again.

My reasons for saying this are based on experience in Church councils, and also from parallel experience in business where people in authority sit in committee with subordinates. It is most difficult for either superior or subordinate to forget this relationship and treat the other just as a person who has certain competencies which may be helpful in solving their common problems.

The average priest has to be willing to suppress his professional habit of passing judgment. Though chairman, he must remember he is not speaking "ex cathedra." His effort must be toward permissiveness, withholding his sense of shock at "radical" ideas. He must see others as having real contributions. He needs tact, patience, warmth, and faith in man. His training and experience as priest, teacher, and judge tend to develop other traits.

The layman cannot allow permissiveness to be the signal for anarchy. Nor should revivals of authoritarianism cow him to silence. His attributes should include also tact, patience, warmth and trust, but also a good measure of courage and persistence.

Without the cultivation of these attitudes, the councils will be fruitless. With these attitudes success is possible if the function of the councils is understood. If one person expects only a forum, while another wants decision-making, someone will be disappointed. We need to know the science of group dynamics and how to use it.

JOHN DONNELLY

The Acts of the Apostles tell us how the various parts of the Church can secure "mutual cooperation." When it was brought to the attention of "the Twelve" that "the widows were being neglected" they called "a council" and told the disciples to "select from among you seven men" to carry out this responsibility. As for the Apostles themselves they felt it their duty to devote themselves "to the ministry of the word."

Within the framework of renewal and reform of the Church the community has much greater needs than the feeding of widows. But these needs must be met in the same way: consultation and cooperation between laity and hierarchy. The so-called "Little Council" in St. Louis is a good example of this cooperation. After weeks of intense publicity, guided by the Cardinal's insistence and encouragement, groups of parishioners met weekly for two months to read and discuss Council documents. At the end of this period each group made specific recommendations for parish and diocesan renewal. Then, at each "parish assembly," these proposals were debated, approved, and implemented. Representatives from each parish were chosen to carry parish proposals to the diocesan "Little Council" held later. Dozens of parish structures have been created: PTAs, ecumenical, liturgical, and social action committees. Though of course there is some friction, on the whole priest and layman are working together for a renewed Church and world. Hopefully this movement will lead to the national and international meetings urged by the Council. The layman has to be made to feel that he is part of the mission of the Church. The "Little Councils" fill that need.

RORY V. ELLINGER

*T*he common heritage of the Scriptures, and the common duty to give Christian witness that flows from this, recommends and often demands the cooperation of Catholics with other Christians on the national and international levels, this by Church communities as well as by individuals, and in permanent organizations as well as on particular projects.[9]

27.

On cooperating with other Christians and with non-Christians

Common human values also frequently call for a similar cooperation between Christians who are pursuing apostolic goals, and others who do not profess Christianity but acknowledge the same values.

This dynamic and prudent cooperation[10] is of great importance in secular activities. Through it lay people give witness both to Christ the redeemer of the world, and to the solidarity of the human family.

*For there is no distinction between Jew and Greek,
for there is the same Lord of all, rich toward all
who call upon him (Rom. 10:12).*

COMMENT

Christ assigned the Apostles to build a movement which could open the love of all men. After two thousand years of dedicated labor the Apostles, and their successors, lay and clerical, have not been able to accomplish this assignment through preaching and conversion.

Now a broader approach is developing. Instead of seeking converts to Catholicism, the contemporary apostle will seek to join with his fellow men to convert the world to peace, order, and justice, and thereby to create the environment of love. Such a method may come much closer to fulfilling Christ's command than proselytizing, and do it with greater freedom and respect for the human person.

In America the real world is urban, complex, violent, pregnant with human potential. Out of this world can come a great society, that is a society of love and order. The building of this society is a task for many men possessed of many talents. Sect, like race, is irrelevant to this building. Generosity, commitment, persistence, these are the relevant criteria for leadership.

Who but a million men of courage, skill, and good will can take the thousand steps necessary in every field of human activity to bring us closer to the good society? Of what use, of what need, is there to ask more about those willing to join the struggle? Their religion? Their birthplace? Their wealth? These can be diverse wellsprings of strength, but they cannot be criteria for separation, otherwise our society, rather than great, will be feeble and fragmented.

It is in the sense of community that flows from such building that man, whether he be Christian or non-Christian, generates the love to restore all things.

JAMES V. CUNNINGHAM, JR.

It is significant that this article's recommendation, and even demand for cooperation with other Christians both as individuals and as church communities is grounded in the Scriptures and their call to witness. I interpret this to mean the cooperation of laymen in the study of the Scriptures as suggested through living-room dialogues, as well as more formal study with biblical scholars. This possibility has been enhanced by a common text and assumes that corporate actions will proceed from a deeper source than human cooperation and good will.

This article opens up almost limitless possibilities for common action since it suggests even permanent organizations to deal with ongoing human problems. The world desperately needs this Christian witness to the reconciliation of God with man and men with one another. One of the tragedies of our divisions has been that our own lack of unity has obscured and sometimes denied before the world the power of Christian faith and love to break the barriers of class, race, and culture which lead to hostility among men and nations.

Laymen, praying, studying, and working together may now forge ahead with a great variety of programs for the alleviation of suffering, the increase of justice, and the building of understanding and good will among men.

In some areas cooperation also becomes possible with non-Christians of good will. Such action may well bring all Christians closer to one another as well as into new relationships of understanding with all men. Most important, it will enable both Catholic and non-Catholic Christians to express more fully and fruitfully what it means to be "the people of God"—Christ's apostolate in the world.

EDGAR H. S. CHANDLER

At a time when more and more Catholics are cooperating with other Christians and non-Christians in very vital ways (community organization, civil rights movement, Peace Corps, inner-city tutoring, anti-poverty programs) there is an urgent need to develop greater sensitivity to the depth of ecumenical relationships. Many Catholics at Selma (to cite one example) shared the feeling that the Church never seems so much the people of God as when it is striving with other members of God's family to make the temporal order more truly human.

When Christians of various communions and non-Christians of varied persuasions, being guided by the highest lights of their consciences, struggle together to remove injustice, secure freedom, and promote deeper understanding and mutual respect, then they are collaborating with the Holy Spirit in building a community of love. And in this joint effort, are they not actually united in the mystical Christ who is in the process of becoming?

Some are so convinced of this already existing unity in Christ that they believe there are occasions when such cooperating Christians and non-Christians could aptly celebrate their unity with Christ's eucharistic feast and sacrifice.

I am not in any way urging uncanonical eucharistic practices, but I am pointing out that there is sometimes a depth in the ecumenical secular relationship, wherein we sense our ultimate unity and discover the holy in the common, Christ in the community, God in man.

WILLIAM G. KRUSE

VI
Formation for the apostolate

28.
The need for formation

*T*he apostolate can be fully effective only if there is a multi-faceted and integrated preparation for it. The steady spiritual and doctrinal progress of lay people themselves, and the variety of persons, tasks, and environments to which their efforts must be adapted, both require such preparation. This formation should be based on the principles expressed in other conciliar declarations and statements.[1] Beyond the formation common to all Christians, many forms of the apostolate require special and specific training, due to the variety of persons and circumstances involved.

29.
The principles of formation for lay people

*L*ay people have their own role in the Church's mission. Therefore their apostolic formation takes on a distinctive quality from the specific and peculiar character of lay life and the spirituality proper to it. Apostolic formation presupposes an integrated human formation in keeping with the talents and situation of each person. For the lay person should thoroughly understand the modern secular world. He ought to be involved in his own society and capable of adjusting himself to its specific character and culture.

But first of all the lay person must have a living faith in the divine mystery of creation and redemption; he must be moved by the Holy Spirit, who enlivens the people of God and urges all·men to love God the Father and in him the secular order and its citizens. That is essential in learning how to carry out the mission of Christ and his Church. Such a formation should be considered the necessary basis for any effective apostolate.

Beyond this spiritual formation, the lay person needs a thorough understanding of doctrine and even a knowledge of philosophy, ethics, and theology suited to each one's talents, age, and circumstances. The importance of general culture, too, as well as practical and technical training, cannot be overlooked.

To further good relations with all men, lay people should respect truly human values, especially those related to living and working in brotherhood with others and establishing dialogue with them.

However, apostolic formation cannot be limited to purely theoretical instruction. Slowly indeed, and carefully, but from the very beginning of his formation, the lay person must learn to look at reality with the eyes of faith, make judgments about it, and act on them. By active involvement he forms and perfects himself in the company of others, and thus embarks on active service to the Church.[2] Moreover, the increasing maturity of the human personality and the complexity of modern problems require that this formation be a continuing one, leading to constantly higher levels of knowledge and corresponding action. In meeting the requirements of such a formation, the integrity and unity of the human personality must be respected and pains taken to preserve and increase its balance and harmony.

With such a formation the lay person can involve himself vigorously and completely in the reality of the secular order and effectively undertake his role in its affairs. At the same time he is a living member and witness of the Church, and makes her actively present to the secular order.[3]

Have this mind in you which was also in Christ Jesus
(Philipp. 2:5).

COMMENT

Nothing has hobbled our understanding of apostolic formation quite so thoroughly as the twin tendency to associate it with an accepted pattern of religious formation or an educational curriculum.

Useful as some elements of a particular religious formation might be, the two "formations" are quite diverse in aim and starting point. A religious community can begin with a novitiate period, presuming a prior decision of the candidate to identify with this religious group. And it will continue to foster that identification as a part of the novice's growth in Christ. An apostolic group looks rather for persons not yet decided but natively generous and capable of concern. Its aim is to develop them in evangelical judgment and secular skills. The group will become an invaluable support but never a key to one's identity.

Similarly, formation in skills and judgment cannot be confused with an educational program — if only because both successfully elude the best-constructed programs. Moreover, the tendency of educators to transform a rhythmical life-process into a linear pattern where certain things "must come first" is inimical to the genius of group life. The "lay person must [indeed] have a living faith in the divine mystery of creation and redemption" — but this will have to grow. And it *will* grow, through an involvement in the needs of others, an involvement which will be slow because it is genuine, though it may not be as "careful" as some may wish. But that is the price of life and of love. Apostolic formation is learning how to risk, so when one pushes through to find that faith which *is* the basis, he will be ready to sacrifice all and embrace it—and with it the world that God so loves.

DAVID B. BURRELL, C.S.C.

When the article says that apostolic formation "presupposes" an integrated human formation, it is saying something vitally important yet something that could be misunderstood. It is true there will be very little profound apostolic formation without integrated human formation, but sometimes, especially in our day, one must be careful not to presuppose that integrated human formation *is* there. Frequently, the beginning of formation consists in helping the person to attain some sort of an integrated human formation. In other words, many people today need help with such human problems as learning to think, making decisions, controlling their will, and, above all, controlling and coping with their emotions. These people are good people. They will make good apostles, but they have problems in their humanity. Grace builds on nature and does not destroy it or even ignore it.

The article's mention of respect for truly human values reminds one of the importance of listening, an art that is, strangely enough, lost today. One listens when one respects. A well-known psychiatrist made a statement shortly before his death that, after all his years in psychiatry, both as a practicing professional and as a teacher, the one and only conclusion that he was really completely sure of was that *people today need someone to listen to them.* This is the beginning of dialogue.

Finally, in some ways, the last part of this article might have been the first part, because it is so fundamental. The see, judge, and act method, conceived by Thomas Aquinas, activated by Cardinal Cardijn, and canonized by Pope John XXIII, is indeed a continuing process and a discovery that is invaluable to the layman. It keeps the lay person with his feet in the order of reality and his head and heart in the realm of faith.

FRANCIS N. WENDELL, O.P.

The words "see-judge-act" sound almost magical, but they demand hard work. Unless people really "see" — get out to meet people, listen to them, look at their community, their city—they will never meet the problems a Christian must affect. Unless they learn to "judge" — to think, to read, find principles to guide their actions, study the doctrine of the Church —their discussions will be superficial and little or no growth will result. Unless there is "action"— doing something to change a situation, become involved with society—they will have missed the greatest force in this technique for formation. If developed properly these steps become a natural way of thinking and acting.

The decree also mentions ". . . the lay person must have a living faith. . . ." Here we face a serious problem. This "living faith" cannot be presupposed to exist; it has to be developed along with and as part of the involvement in the temporal order. People have to experience Christ—in Scripture, in the liturgy, particularly the Mass. They have to experience Christian community—in worship, in meetings, in beer-drinking. In cases where we have seen this "formation" take place, a dedicated chaplain was generally the spark helping these people develop a love for Christ and their fellow man. But the number of priests interested and willing to help in this formation are few. How can we find, or develop, priests who will accept this challenge of learning how to give lay people this "living faith" that will be the foundation for their action? Or is the future in the hands of lay people who will themselves develop other lay people?

MR. AND MRS. DONALD O'CONNELL

30.

Forming others for the apostolate

*A*postolic formation should begin with the earliest instruction of childhood. However, special emphasis should be placed on orienting adolescents and young people to the apostolate and filling them with its spirit. As new responsibilities are assumed, this formation should be continued through the whole life-span. It is therefore obvious that those who supervise Christian education are also bound to offer training for the apostolate.

In the family, parents should orient their children to recognize God's love for all men. Gradually, and by example especially, they must teach them to be concerned about the material and spiritual needs of their neighbor. The whole family and its habits of life thus become a sort of novitiate for the apostolate.

Children should be educated, too, to see beyond the confines of the family and open their minds to the community, both of the Church and of the secular world. They should be so assimilated into the community life of their local parish that they thereby acquire an awareness of themselves as living, active members of the people of God. Further, priests in their work as catechists, preachers, spiritual directors, and in other pastoral functions, should pay attention to the apostolic formation of their people.

Schools, colleges, and other Catholic educational institutions should encourage in young people a genuinely Catholic attitude toward apostolic activity. Where this formation is for any reason lacking, as in the case of children who do not attend such schools, it is all the more important for parents, pastors, and apostolic organizations to remedy the defect. On the other hand, teachers and educators, who by their very state in life are involved in an outstanding form of the lay apostolate, should have such competence in doctrinal content and pedagogical techniques that they can transmit this training effectively.

Lay associations and organizations, whether directed to the apostolate or other supernatural purposes, should likewise give earnest and diligent encouragement to formation for the apostolate, as their resources and objectives permit.[4] Often they are the normal means for a realistic apostolic formation, since they can offer a training in doctrine at once spiritual and practical. Their members can meet in small groups with associates and friends to assess the techniques and results of their apostolic work and to relate the context of their daily lives to the teachings of the Gospel.

Apostolic formation should be so directed that account is taken of the entire range of the lay person's apostolate. This apostolate is not limited to the activity of associations and organizations but is to be exercised in all the situations and contexts of life, with emphasis on professional and social life. Each person should be energetically devoted to his own apostolic formation, particularly so in his adult years. For with maturity the mind becomes more open and a person can more accurately measure his own God-given talents; this makes possible a more effective use of the charisms which the Holy Spirit has imparted to each one for the advantage of his brothers.

I am in labor again until Christ is found in you
(Gal. 4:19).

COMMENT

The great sums spent on Catholic education in the United States are concentrated on less than half of the Catholic school-age population. Most school-age Catholics attend public schools— well over 5 per cent is a conservative estimate. Almost none of the Church's budget for education is directed to the Christian education and apostolic formation of these students. This leads to the question: Are we really serious about the majority of our Catholic youth? Many of them may attend their one-hour-a-week CCD program. But can such a program give a systematic religious education and the kind of apostolic formation of which the Decree speaks? With seven days between classes, and home-study practically non-existent, can a subject really be learned? It could be that we are devoting much effort to what is pedagogically unsound.

The orderly presentation of religious doctrines, which characterizes a planned course in religion, needs to be coupled with action, discovery, liturgical celebrations, and, above all, the experience of Christian faith. This means that students must feel that they are linked to one another by mutual faith. They need to discover Christ in their midst forming them into a community of faith, hope, and charity. Until they are able to share together this experience of Christian faith, the climate which fosters Christian education and apostolic formation is not present. Practically, what steps can be taken? Perhaps several hours several days a week; a more personal bond between teacher and student; teacher-student relationships in apostolic experiences; more opportunity to discuss, to observe, and to become involved in situations which make religious truths come to life.

THEODORE C. STONE

The overall impression conveyed by this article is one of a genuine advance toward the new and much needed contemporary theology and psychology of Christian education which is embedded in many of the Council documents. Education is equated, as it should be, with a whole life-development. It is also inserted into all of human activity, not merely the formally intellectual, as for example classroom teaching. The acquiring of apostolic attitudes like generosity and service, as well as apostolic techniques like group discussion, are considered integral and essential for any adequate Christian formation in the post-conciliar world.

Paragraph 4 is the weakest of the article. It resorts to the old use of rhetoric about encouraging young people to be apostolic. No one ever became anything, least of all an apostle, without years of study, planning, and example from those more advanced, as well as hard and consistent experience. This paragraph also implies the old bias that somehow Catholic schools do something to their students automatically, which those not attending Catholic schools lack as a "defect." This seems an unreal approach to Christian formation, with a majority of Catholics in non-Catholic institutions and the Catholic schools themselves in a turmoil of questioning and needed experimentation. Those staffing schools potentially play a part in formation, but they do not "transmit" it.

The most important stress in the article is the strong statement on the value and necessity of group discussion and action based on common study of the Gospels. The true key to vital and lasting apostolic formation, as presented at length by Pope John in *Mater et Magistra,* is precisely this group experience. Only in group thought and action can the Christian of

any age and ability be formed in community life and experience Christ in such a meaningful way that he will be desirous and able to act as an apostle.

SISTER CHARLES BORROMEO, C.S.C.

To form others for the apostolate we must be conscious of the fact that we do this not so much by what we say but rather what we do and even more by what we are. We must truly love the people "we" (really it is the Holy Spirit) are forming. Children especially sense this very keenly. This is our first step—to accept them and love them as they are. Then we patiently dispose them so that they will be open for the action of the Holy Spirit.

The "orientation of adolescents and young people to the apostolate" will best be achieved by making it possible for them to *discover* their role in the apostolate. We should use induction rather than deduction. Start with something of interest in their lives and then through discussion they will discover their role. They do not want to be told "You must do this and that and be a good apostle." Rather we are more effective if we question them to clarify *their* thinking.

There is a big difference between giving students formation and giving information. Many have their religion in their memory and not in their heart. Formation means development, advancing in Christ-likeness in leadership, and in action. It does not mean leaving the world but rather "to christianize the world exactly as it is being built." Formation means bringing Christ who was at Cana to the high school prom; the realization that Christ who spoke to the disciples on the way to Emmaus speaks to adolescents and young people on the way to the drive-in theatre.

R. G. FITZPATRICK

31.
Adjusting this formation to various apostolates

*T*he various forms of the apostolate require specific and comparable kinds of formation:

a) Regarding the apostolate of evangelizing and sanctifying men, lay people should be specially trained to initiate dialogue with others, both believers and non-believers, in order to witness Christ's message to all.[5]

Since we are currently witnessing a new kind of materialism which is generally pervasive, even among Catholics, lay people should be even more earnest in understanding Christian teaching, especially on controversial matters. And more important, they should oppose every form of materialism by the witness of a life lived according to the Gospels.

b) Regarding the Christian renewal of the secular order, lay people should be thoroughly instructed about the genuine meaning and value of secular things, both as self-contained realities and as they relate to the final goals of human life. They should be knowledgeable about the organizing of institutions and the intelligent use of secular things, with unremitting concern for the public welfare in accordance with the Church's moral and social teachings. The principles of her social doctrine, and the conclusions to which they lead, are to be so thoroughly assimilated by lay people that they become competent not only to apply that teaching intelligently to specific situations, but to take their own share in the further development of that doctrine.[6]

c) Since the most vivid witness of Christian life is afforded by the works of mercy and charity, the faithful should be taught from childhood to share the sufferings of their brothers and to assist them generously when in need.[7]

I became all things to all men that I might save all
(1 Cor. 9:22).

COMMENT

A note of genuine respect for "secular things" is apparent in article 31. This is all to the good, as the Church generally, and the lay apostolate specifically, have not made a complete escape from the notion that "the world" is somehow tainted and not worthy of our best efforts. Even thirty-five years after *Quadragesimo Anno,* and despite the magnificent world-vision of *Mater et Magistra* and *Pacem in Terris,* many Christians still regard the world as a necessary evil, to be endured patiently until the Second Coming.

Some lay apostolic groups, however, have anticipated this article. "Incarnational spirituality" has become a consecrated phrase in the literature of certain Catholic Action organizations. A layman lives and works in the world, as the manuals put it; it is here, in the framework of his daily life, in his coming to grips with the world and its problems, in his facing up to the possibilities of complex modern living that he grows as a person in and through Christ. He learns not merely to accept the secular sphere, but to value and cherish it as the proper arena for his creative action in fulfilling his co-redemptive role.

The presence of Catholics in community organizations, in political life, in urban renewal programs, on village school boards, in civil rights groups, in anti-poverty campaigns is an encouraging sign. Competence in these fields is essential, of course, and the article underscores this. But the Church's crying need, even at this late date, is for Christians who realize that they must live in the real world.

LAURENCE KELLY

When article 31 says that ". . . lay people should be thoroughly instructed about the genuine meaning and value of secular things..," it seems to imply that those responsible for directing this formation already know the genuine meaning and value of secular things and, furthermore, that they know how secular values relate to the basic goals of human life; "formation" also suggests that this knowledge can be poured into people. One gets the impression that the objective is to produce an army of lay people who have all been trained to move in step with their leaders, rather than to help lay people develop as responsible, mature Christians exercising their personal freedom and individual initiative.

The article as a whole raises several questions:

Are the distinctions it makes between the forms of the apostolate valid ones? Can the Christian life be so neatly compartmentalized?

Why is training lay people to initiate dialogue referred to as the apostolate of evangelizing? Does this mean dialogue with other Christians and non-believers is for the purpose of gaining converts? Why is the issue of materialism coupled in the same sentence with the statement that "lay people should be even more earnest in understanding Christian teaching, especially on controversial matters"? Is the assumption here that controversial issues can be reduced to a simple polemic, with Christian teachings on one hand and "materialism" on the other? The article refers to Christian renewal of the secular order. Are there not secular values that have something to offer Christian renewal?

Finally, does not the exhortation to give vivid witness of Christian life by works of mercy and charity seem to be a mere appendage? Should not, rather, a spirit of mercy and charity permeate the Christian life of dialogue with other men and the process of developing a human society?

VAILE SCOTT

Numerous resources are already available, such as seminars, conventions, retreats, days of recollection, conferences, books, and lectures; all these can help the lay person dedicated to the apostolate to arrive at a deeper knowledge of Scripture and Christian teaching. They will help him also to improve his spiritual life, to understand the secular situation, and to discover and develop effective techniques for the apostolate.[8]

32.

The means to be used

These resources should take account of the various forms of the apostolate and the environments in which it must be exercised. For the same end, centers of study and higher institutes have also been founded, and already produce excellent results. This holy synod is delighted by undertakings of this nature, which are already successful in some countries, and desires their establishment in other places where they are needed. Moreover we urge the establishment of centers for research and study, not only in theology, but also in anthropology, psychology, sociology, and methodology, so that for all the areas of the apostolate the talents of lay people, men and women, youth and adults, may be better developed.

Final exhortation

33.

This holy council earnestly exhorts in the Lord all lay people to give a glad, generous, and prompt response to the inspiration of the Holy Spirit and to the voice of Christ who, at this hour, invites them even more insistently. Let our young people feel that this summons is directed in a special way to them. May they accept the summons with eagerness and generosity.

For through this holy synod the Lord himself over and over again invites all lay people to an increasingly intimate union with himself. He invites them to recognize that what is his is also theirs (see Phil. 2:5) and wishes them to associate themselves with him in his mission of redemption. He is sending them forth again to go ahead of Him to every town and place where He intends to visit personally (see Luke 10:1) so that in the many forms and expressions of the one apostolate of the Church, which is constantly to be renewed to meet modern needs, they may show themselves to be his fellow-workers, devoting themselves fully at all times to the Lord's work, realizing that their toil in the Lord can never be in vain (see 1 Cor. 15:58).

Therefore, my beloved brethren, be steadfast . . .
abounding in the work of the Lord, knowing that
your labor is not in vain in the Lord (1 Cor. 15:58).

COMMENT

The means suggested for helping the layman to know more about Scripture and Christian teaching are available now, since many teachers are already prepared. But if the layman is to learn how to "improve his spiritual life, understand the secular situation, and discover and develop effective techniques for the apostolate," there must be a crash program to teach teachers. Laymen will not be effectively formed except by laymen; we need once more Cardinal Cardijn's technique of "like to like." Laymen who are now qualified, therefore, should be writing, lecturing, teaching courses, supplementing the work of retreat-masters, in an all-out effort to increase their own numbers. Already many laymen are studying theology with a view to teaching it; others are preparing to engage in a full-time apostolate in the missions or in parishes at home. They must be multiplied so that a consensus of lay spirituality for the twentieth (and twenty-first) century may emerge—not an ill-tailored version of sanctuary or cloister spirituality, but one that takes into account such realities as marriage, children, a home of one's own, bills, neighbors, shopping, school, insurance, health, and with it and through it all a listening to the Gospel as it was preached to laymen.

Can this be done on the university level? The Council says it can, and urges the establishment of interdisciplinary research centers. Swifter, perhaps, might be the gathering together of high school and college graduates, already well grounded in the faith, into study groups, Catholic Action cells, professional sodalities, and the like, for the pooling of ideas, plans, projects, for tireless dialogue and discussion. There is an untapped reservoir of brains and zeal here. In the past thirty years those in this reservoir have been too dependent on clerical supervision. Put on its own by the Council, and given scope by pastors—who must be willing to risk an occasional mistake—such a reservoir could provide for the laity streams of the water that leaps up into eternal life.

WILLIAM J. LEONARD, S.J.

What do we mean, by the expression found in this article, "to improve his spiritual life"? Certainly not the multiplication of devotional practices; but, rather, a dynamically transforming understanding of salvation in the contemporary world. That this formation should have for its end a grasp of the "secular situation" is most important. For this can hardly be conceived of as a by-product of an ecclesiastical or religious culture (as article 31 suggests). This education overflows into action: "discover and develop effective techniques for the apostolate." But let us not divorce techniques from principles. What we must aim for, first, is the formation of lay apostles who will first recognize, analyze, and interpret the milieu, the situation, and then adopt or adapt the appropriate techniques.

Article 32 points out two types of structures for formation: occasional, or passing, and permanent. Let us emphasize the importance of the permanent and more profound: centers of study and graduate schools. The long-term formation they offer is deep enough to prepare laymen for positions of leadership in the apostolate, not merely for the performing of secondary tasks assigned by the clergy.

Such centers of study are to be found already in several parts of the world, under various titles—cathechetical, pastoral, liturgical, social—catering to a student body made up of laymen, religious, and priests. Following the Council these will be multiplied. And it is to be hoped they will be found offering to an increasing number of laymen an ever-deepening formation, calling upon new and original methods.

The content of this formation ought to be doctrinal, of course, imparting a thorough knowledge of the sacred sciences, but also anthropological, that is integrating the humanistic sciences.

Could we not take advantage of the resources available in secular universities? Laymen with an adequate theological and philosophical background might follow the courses of eminent professors in secular settings either concurrently with, or after, their theological preparation. The unifying synthesis between Christian formation and humanistic and scientific studies could be assured through seminars where the apostolic experience would take its place along with the other objects of sociological and psychological research.

JOSEPH BOURNIQUE

Footnotes

Introduction

1—Cf. John XXIII, apostolic constitution "Humani Salutis," Dec. 25, 1961: A.A.S. 54 (1962) pp. 7-10.

2—Cf. Second Vatican Council, Dogmatic Constitution on the Nature of the Church, nos. 33 ff.: A.A.S. 57 (1965) pp. 39 ff.; cf. also Constitution on the Liturgy, nos. 26-40; A.A.S. 56 (1964) pp. 107-111; cf. Decree on Instruments of Social Communication: A.A.S. 56 (1964) pp. 145-158; cf. Decree on Ecumenism: A.A.S. 57 (1965) pp. 90-107; cf. Decree on Pastoral Duties of Bishops, nos. 16, 17, 18; cf. Declaration on Christian Education, nos. 3, 5, 7; cf. Decree on Missionary Activity of Church, nos. 15, 21, 41; cf. Decree on Priestly Life and Ministry, no. 9.

3—Cf. Pius XII, allocution to cardinals, Feb. 18, 1946: A.A.S. 38 (1946) pp. 101-102; Idem., sermon to Young Christian Workers, Aug. 25, 1957; A.A.S. 49 (1957) p. 843.

Chapter I

1—Cf. Pius XI, encyclical "Rerum Ecclesiae": A.A.S. 18 (1926) p. 65.

2—Cf. Second Vatican Council, Dogmatic Constitution on the Nature of the Church, no. 31: A.A.S. 57 (1965) p. 37.

3—Cf. Ibid., no. 33, p. 39; cf. also no. 10, ibid., p. 14.

4—Cf. Ibid., no. 12, p. 16.

5—Cf. Second Vatican Council, Constitution on the Liturgy, Chap. 1, no. 11: A.A.S. 56 (1964) pp. 102-103.

6—Cf. Second Vatican Council, Dogmatic Constitution on the Nature of the Church, no. 32: A.A.S. 57 (1965) p. 38; cf. also nos. 40-41: ibid., pp. 45-47.

7—Ibid., no. 62, p. 63; cf. also no. 65, ibid., pp. 64-65.

Chapter II

1—Cf. Pius XI, encyclical "Ubi Arcano," Dec. 23, 1922: A.A.S. 14 (1922) p. 659; Pius XII, encyclical "Summi Pontificatus," Oct. 20, 1939: A.A.S. 31 (1939) pp. 442-443.

2—Cf. Leo XIII, encyclical "Rerum Novarum:" A.A.S. 23 (1890-91) p. 47; Pius XI encyclical "Quadragesimo anno:" A.A.S. 23 (1931) p. 190; Pius XII, radio message of June 1, 1941: A.A.S. 33 (1941) p. 207.

3—Cf. John XXIII, encyclical "Mater et Magistra": A.A.S. 53 (1961) p. 402.

4—Cf. ibid., pp. 440-441.

5—Cf. ibid., pp. 442-443.

6—Cf. Pius XII, allocution to "Pax Romana" April 25, 1957: A.A.S. 49 (1957) pp. 298-299; and especially John XXIII, "Ad Conventum Consilii" Food and Agriculture Organization Nov. 10, 1959: A.A.S. 51 (1959) pp. 856-866.

Chapter III

1—Cf. St. Pius X, apostolic letter "Creationis Duarum Novarum Paroeciarum" June 1, 1905: A.A.S. 38 (1905) pp. 65-67; Pius XII, allocution to faithful of parish of St. Saba, Jan. 11, 1953: Discourses and Radio Messages of His Holiness Pius XII, 14 (1952-53) pp. 449-454; John XXIII, allocution to clergy and faithful of suburbicarian diocese of Albano, "Ad Arcem Gandulfi Habita," Aug. 26, 1962: A.A.S. 54 (1962) pp. 656-660.

2—Cf. Leo XIII, allocution Jan. 28, 1894: Acts, 14 (1894) pp. 424-425.

3—Cf. Pius XII, allocution to pastors, etc., Feb. 6, 1951: Discourses and Radio Messages of His Holiness Pius XII, 12 (1950-51) pp. 437-443; 852: ibid., 14 (1952-53) pp. 5-10; March 27, 1953: ibid., 15 (1953-54) pp. 27-35; Feb. 28, 1954: ibid., pp. 585-590.

4—Cf. Pius XI, encyclical "Casti Connubii": A.A.S. 22 (1930) p. 554; Pius XII, Radio Messages, Jan. 1, 1941: A.A.S. 33 (1941) p. 203; idem., to delegates of the convention of the members of the International Union to Protect the Rights of Families, Sept. 20, 1949: A.A.S. 41 (1949) p. 552; idem., to heads of families on pilgrimage from France to Rome, Sept. 18, 1951: A.A.S. 43 (1951) p. 731, idem., Christmas Radio Message of 1952: A.A.S. 45 (1953) p. 41; John XXIII, encyclical "Mater et Magistra" May 15, 1961: A.A.S. (1961) pp. 429, 439.

5—Cf. Pius XII, encyclical "Evangelii Praecones," June 2, 1951: A.A.S. 43 (1951) p. 514.

6—Cf. Pius XII, to delegates to the convention of members of the International Union for the Defense of Family Rights, Sept. 20, 1949: A.A.S. 41 (1949) p. 552.

7—Cf. St. Pius X, allocution to Association of French Catholic Youth on piety, knowledge and action, Sept. 25, 1904: A.A.S. 37 (1904-05) pp. 296-300.

8—Cf. Pius XII, letter "Dans Quelques Semaines" to Archbishop of Montreal, Canada, to be relayed to the Assemblies of Canadian Young Christian Workers, May 24, 1947: A.A.S. 39 (1947) p. 257; radio message to Young Christian Workers, Brussels, Sept. 3, 1950: A.A.S. 42 (1950) pp. 640-641.

9—Cf. Pius XI, encyclical "Quadragesimo Anno," May 15, 1931: A.A.S. 23 (1931) pp. 225-226.

10—Cf. John XXIII, encyclical "Mater et Magistra" May 15, 1961: A.A.S. 53 (1961) pp. 448-450.

Chapter IV

1—Cf. Pius XII, allocution to the first convention of laymen representing all nations on the promotion of the apostolate, Oct. 15, 1951: A.A.S 43 (1951) p. 788.

2—Cf. Pius XII, allocution to the first convention of laymen representing all nations on the promotion of the apostolate, Oct. 15, 1951: A.A.S 43 (1951) pp. 787-788.

3—Cf. Pius XII, encyclical "Le Pelerinage de Lourdes," July 2, 1957 A.A.S. 49 (1957) p. 615.

4—Cf. Pius XII, allocution to the assembly of the International Federation of Catholic Men, Dec. 8, 1956 A.A.S. 49 (1957) pp. 26-27.

5—Cf. Sacred Congregation of the Council, concerning the dissolution of the Corrientes diocese in Argentina Nov. 13, 1920: A.A.S. 13 (1921) p 139.

6—Cf. in Chap. 5, no. 24.

7—Cf. John XXIII, encyclical "Princeps Pastorum," Dec. 10, 1959 A.A.S. 51 (1959) p. 856.

8—Cf. Pius XI, letter "Quae Nobis" to Cardinal Bertram, Nov. 13, 1928 A.A.S. 20 (1928) p. 385. Cf. also Pius XII, allocution to Italian Catholic Action, Sept. 4, 1940: A.A.S. 3 (1940) p. 362.

Chapter V

1—Cf. Pius XI, encyclical "Quam vis Nostra," April 30, 1936: A.A.S 28 (1936) pp. 160-161.

2—Cf. Sacred Congregation of the Council on the dissolution of the diocese of Corrientes, Argentina, Nov. 13, 1920; A.A.S. 13 (1921) pp. 137 140.

3—Cf. Pius XII, allocution to the second convention of laymen representing all nations on the promotion of the apostolate, Oct. 5, 1957: A.A.S. 49 (1957) p. 927.

4—Cf. Second Vatican Council, Dogmatic Constitution on the Nature of the Church, no. 37: A.A.S. 5 (1965) pp. 442-443.

5—Cf. Pius XII, apostolic exhortation "Menti Nostrae," Sept. 23, 1950 A.A.S. 42 (1950) p. 660.

6—Cf. Second Vatican Council, Decree on the Renovation of Religious Life, no. 8.

7—Cf. Benedict XIV, On the Dio-san Synod, I, 3, Chap. 9, no. 7.

8—Cf. Pius XI, encyclical "Quam-s Nostra," April 30, 1936: A.A.S. (1936) pp. 160-161.

9—Cf. John XXIII, encyclical "Ma-r et Magistra," May 15, 1961: A.A.S. 53 (1961) pp. 456-457. Cf. econd Vatican Council, Decree on cumenism, no. 12: A.A.S. 57 (1965) . 99-100.

10—Cf. Second Vatican Council, ecree on Ecumenism, no. 12: A.A.S. (1965) p. 100. Also Cf. Dogmatic onstitution on the Nature of the hurch, no. 15: A.A.S. 57 (1965) pp. -20.

Chapter VI

1—Cf. Second Vatican Council, ogmatic Constitution on the Nature the Church, Chaps. 2, 4 and 5: A.A.S. 57 (1965) pp. 12-21, 37-49; so Cf. Decree on Ecumenism, nos. 6, 7 and 12: A.A.S. 57 (1965) pp. , 96, 97, 99, 100; Cf. also above, . 4.

2—Cf. Pius XII, allocution to the rst international Boy Scouts con-ress, June 6, 1952: A.A.S. 44 (1952) . 579-580; John XXIII, encyclical, Mater et Magistra," May 15, 1961: A.A.S. 53 (1961) p. 456.

3—Cf. Second Vatican Council, ogmatic Constitution on the Nature the Church, p. 33: A.A.S. 57 1965) p. 39.

4—Cf. John XXIII, encyclical "Ma-r et Magistra," May 15, 1961: A.A.S. 53 (1961) p. 455.

5—Cf. Pius XII, encyclical "Ser-m Laetitiae," Nov. 1, 1939: A.A.S. (1939) pp. 653-654; Cf. Idem., to aduates of Italian Catholic Action, ay 24, 1953.

6—Cf. Pius XII, allocution to the niversal congress of the World Fed-ation of Young Catholic Women, pril 18, 1952: A.A.S. 42 (1952) pp. 4-419. Cf. idem., allocution to the hristian Association of Italian orkers, May 1, 1955: A.A.S. 47 1955) pp. 403-404.

7—Cf. Pius XII, to delegates of e Assembly of Charity Associations, pril 27, 1952: pp. 470-471.

8—Cf. John XXIII, encyclical "Ma-r et Magistra," May 15, 1961: A.A.S. 53 (1961) p. 454.

Discussion Questions

Introduction

1. How is the place of laymen integral or essential to the mission of the Church? In introducing the Decree why does the Council consider first and in three times as lengthy a fashion the layman's task in the world before taking up the layman's priest-helper role?

Chapter I

2. How would a layman act as "yeast" if he had the type of employment you have?

3. What kinds of charisms do you think you see in the lives of laymen around you? In yourself?

4. When liturgy and family life, or liturgy and leisure are compartmentalized, what specific effects does this have in these areas of our life?
   What qualities do you expect to see in an authentically lay spirituality that you do not expect to see in the spirituality of a priest or religious?

Chapter II

5. Do we usually think more in terms of the salvation of individuals than renewal of the world? If we do, why is this so?

6. How can lay people apply Christian principles to the problems they see?

7. Distinguish the role of the layman from the role of the pastor in respect to secular realities. How would this distinction apply in the activities of community organizations or of local government?

8. Give an example from your own experience of how a layman's "witness of love" was a sign of Christ's messianic mission. What was the "sign" value of this witness?

Chapter III

9. Can you think of some specific ways in which lay women could participate more intensively in apostolic action?

10. How can parish organizations be renewed so that laymen can bring their real problems and those of the world into the open there?

11. How can the average Christian couple be trained to give a better, more varied witness of Christ to the world?

12. Does the Council see the youth apostolate primarily as training young people for a future adult role or does it see it more as preparing them for a genuinely significant mission as children or youth? Explain.

13. Why is social action so much the province and function of laymen that it should scarcely ever be undertaken by priests or religious?

14. Does every Christian layman have a national and international apostolate of his own? Give examples of the sort of apostolic opportunities open to the average layman in national and international life.

Chapter IV

15. Why is it important that lay people be free to exercise both an individual and an organized apostolate?

16. See if you can find the six varieties of the individual apostolate mentioned in the text and ask yourself whether each is appropriate in your own life and environment.

17. Why is the Council concerned about the danger of isolation of Christians?

18. The Council lists more than ten reasons why organizations can be important. Find them and rate the layman's organization you know best as to whether it is important in these ways.

19. Why does the Council ask us to prize highly, apostolic organizations which work to relate faith and life?
What other goals can apostolic organizations have?

20. Mandated "Catholic Action" groups, as distinguished from free lay apostolate groups, are invited to "verify" their characteristics according to certain criteria (a-d in article 20). In what ways does the Council want the groups renewed?

21. In what concrete ways can Catholic international organizations be promoted and appreciated?

22. What does the Council recommend as just and worthy treatment of professional Catholic laymen and women? In what other ways might their work be adequately recognized?

Chapter V

23. From your own experience, what kinds of dialogue are necessary for apostolic organizations to achieve coordination with the hierarchy and with other forms of the lay apostolate?

24. In what kinds of situations should the lay apostolate be open to proper hierarchical initiatives? Why is this important?

25. Why does the lay apostolate need the competent, brotherly service of apostolic priests and religious? What is the role of the priest in the lay apostolate?

26. As parish, inter-parish, inter-diocesan, national, and international councils are organized, how can the goals of coordination and respect for autonomy and individual characteristics best be achieved?

27. What might a dynamic and prudent cooperation consist of between Catholics, other Christians, and non-Christians?

Chapter VI

28. Why is a multi-faceted formation of laymen needed? What are some of these facets?

29. Why cannot an integrated formation be accomplished merely by achieving a more efficient method of giving theoretical instruction?

30. If parents, parishes, schools, CCD's and other lay organizations are bound to offer apostolic training, what should be done to get started or to achieve greater effectiveness with what is now under way?

31. How can a layman take a personal part in the development of Christian social doctrine?

32. What services could a diocesan lay apostolate research and study center provide for parish, occupational, or problem-centered forms of the lay apostolate?

33. Who actually does the inviting and who is invited to the lay apostolate?

Contributors

MATHEW AHMANN is Executive Director of the National Catholic Conference for Interracial Justice.

JAMES BELANGER is Catechetical Director for St. Bernardine Parish, Forest Park, Ill.

MR. AND MRS. JOSEPH BONSIGNORE are Chairmen of the National Program Committee of the Christian Family Movement.

MSGR. MARVIN BORDELON is pastor of St. Joseph's Parish in Shreveport, La.

FATHER JOSEPH M. BOURNIQUE is Director of the *Institut Pastorale Catechetique* in Paris.

MSGR. EDWARD C. BURKHARDT is Director of the Confraternity of Christian Doctrine for the Archdiocese of Detroit.

FATHER DAVID BURRELL, C.S.C., is a member of the Department of Philosophy at the University of Notre Dame.

MOST REV. CHARLES A. BUSWELL is Bishop of Pueblo, Colorado.

DR. EDGAR H. S. CHANDLER is Executive Director of the Church Federation of Greater Chicago.

JERRY CHARIPAR is a former staff member of the Young Christian Students movement (college).

MSGR. JOSIAH G. CHATHAM is pastor of St. Richard's Parish in Jackson, Miss.

MR. AND MRS. JOHN CIHI are former members of the Young Christian Workers (now Young Christian Movement).

DENNIS CLARK is a staff member of the Center for Community Studies at Temple University.

JAMES J. COCKRELL., JR., is a Tulsa businessman who is lay head of the Oklahoma City-Tulsa Diocese's "Little Council."

YVES CONGAR, O.P., is the author of *Lay People in the Church* and many other theological works.

FATHER JOHN F. CRONIN, S.S., is Assistant Director of the Social Action Department of the National Catholic Welfare Conference.

MR. AND MRS. PATRICK CROWLEY are National Secretary-Couple of the CFM.

JAMES V. CUNNINGHAM, JR., is Director of Neighborhood Urban Extension for ACTION-Housing, Inc., in Pittsburgh.

DOROTHY DAY is editor of *The Catholic Worker* and co-founder of the Catholic Worker movement.

FATHER GODFREY DIEKMANN, O.S.B., is editor-in-chief of *Worship* magazine.

FATHER JOSEPH DILLON is Director of Religious Education for the Diocese of Oklahoma City-Tulsa.

JOHN DONNELLY is President of the National Council of Catholic Men.

RORY ELLINGER is a former National Vice-President of the Newman Foundation.

FATHER R. G. FITZPATRICK is Executive Director of the Office of Religious Education of the Canadian Catholic Conference.

PETER FOOTE is Executive Assistant for the Catholic Action Federations of the Archdiocese of Chicago.

FATHER ROBERT FRANCOEUR is the author of *Perspectives in Evolution* and a member of the faculty at Fairleigh Dickinson University.

FATHER DENNIS GEANEY, O.S.A., author of *You Shall Be Witnesses*, is a well-known writer and lecturer.

FATHER VINCENT J. GIESE is a priest of the Chicago Archdiocese and the former Editorial Director of Fides Publishers.

FATHER DOMENICO GRASSO, S.J., is Director of the Department of Pastoral Theology, Gregorian University, Rome.

DONALD P. GRAY is a member of the Department of Theology at Manhattan College.

FATHER ANDREW GREELEY is a well-known author and Senior Study Director, National Opinion Research Center, Chicago.

MSGR. JOSEPH B. GREMILLION is Director of Socio-Eonomic Development for Catholic Relief Services, NCWC.

DAN HERR is President of the Thomas More Association, Chicago.

FATHER JOHN J. HILL is a priest of the Chicago Archdiocese and co-author of *A Modern Catechism*.

FATHER JOHANNES HOFINGER, S.J., is the Associate Director of the East Asian Pastoral Institute, Manila.

PATRICK KEEGAN was a lay auditor at the Second Vatican Council and is a former International President, YCW.

FATHER JAMES M. KELLER, M.M., is the founder and director of the Christopher Movement.

FATHER LAURENCE KELLY is Chaplain of the Catholic Action Federations of the Archdiocese of Chicago.

FATHER JAMES J. KILLGALLON is a priest of the Chicago Archdiocese and co-author of the *Life in Christ* catechism.

MR. AND MRS. DONALD KRAFT are a former officer-couple of the Chicago CFM.

WILLIAM KRUSE is a former Peace Corps Project Director in Ethiopia and Nigeria.

JUSTUS GEORGE LAWLER is the editor of the quarterly, *Continuum*, and a member of the faculty, St. Xavier College, Chicago.

VIRGINIA LEARY is Training Director for the International Catholic Auxiliaries, Evanston, Ill.

FATHER WILLIAM LEONARD, S.J., is a former officer, National Liturgical Conference.

MOST REV. STEPHEN A. LEVEN is Auxiliary Bishop of San Antonio, Texas.

BERNARD LYONS is Assistant Director of Public Relations for DePaul University.

JOHN MCCUDDEN works as an editor for the Techny Publications Center.

DAVID L. MCMANUS is President of Helicon Publishers.

ROMEO MAIONE, a former International President, YCW, is a staff member of the International Affairs Department of the Canadian Labor Congress.

FATHER H. J. MAJERUS is the CCD Director for the Diocese of New Ulm, Minn.

LOUIS MARRONE is Director of the Neighborhood Centers for the Catholic Adult Education Center of Chicago.

GERALD MISCHE is a co-founder of the Association for International Development.

WILLIAM J. NAGLE works in the U. S. Department of State and is a board member of the National Liturgical Conference.

FATHER WILLIAM F. NERIN is pastor of St. John the Baptist Parish, Edmond, Oklahoma.

FATHER FRANK NORRIS, S.S., is Professor of Theology at St. Patrick's Seminary, Menlo Park, Calif.

MICHAEL NOVAK, author of *Belief and Unbelief*, is a member of the faculty at Stanford University.

MR. AND MRS. DONALD O'CONNELL are CFM President-Couple in the Archdiocese of Milwaukee.

FATHER LOUIS J. PUTZ, C.S.C., is President of Fides Publishers and a member of the Department of Theology at the University of Notre Dame.

MOST REV. VICTOR J. REED is Bishop of the Diocese of Oklahoma City-Tulsa.

WILLIAM REEDY is Head of the Religion Department of the Sadlier Publishing Co.

FATHER H. A. REINHOLD is the author of *Bringing the Liturgy to the People* and many other books and articles on the liturgy.

FATHER JOHN RYAN is a priest of the Diocese of Peoria.

MARY PERKINS RYAN is the author of *Are Parochial Schools Necessary?* and the editor of the catechetical quarterly, *The Living Light*.

BROTHER MICHAEL SALMON is Director of the Little Brothers of Notre Dame in Chicago.

MICHAEL SCHILTZ is an associate editor of *New City* magazine and a Senior Study Director, National Opinion Research Center, Chicago.

VAILE SCOTT is Executive Director of the Catholic Adult Education Center, Chicago.

SISTER CHARLES BORROMEO, C.S.C., is editor of *The Changing Sister* and a member of the Department of Theology at St. Mary's College, Notre Dame, Ind.

SISTER GERTRUDE JOSEPH, C.S.J.O., is the author of *The Sister Apostle* and a member of the National Advisory Board, YCS (high school).

SISTER M. CAROL FRANCES, B.V.M., is Chairman of the Department of Theology at Mundelein College, Chicago.

SISTER MARIE AUGUSTA NEAL, S.N.D., is head of the Sociology Department at Emmanuel College, Boston.

FATHER GERARD S. SLOYAN is Head of the Department of Religious Education at Catholic University, Washington, D.C.

PETER STEINFELS is an assistant editor of *Commonweal* magazine.

FATHER THEODORE STONE is Assistant CCD Director in Chicago and a member of the Executive Committee, National Liturgical Conference.

BARBARA WARD is an economist and the author of *Five Ideas that Change the World* and many other works.

FATHER GERARD P. WEBER, a priest of the Chicago Archdiocese, is the co-author of *The Child and the Christian Mystery* and other books.

FATHER FRANCIS N. WENDELL, O.P., is the author of *The Formation of A Lay Apostle.*

ANTHONY ZIVALICH, a former National President, YCM, is an organizer for the Teamsters Union, Southern Council.

New Departures

WORLD

The Church in the Modern World — Part I • The Church and Man's Calling

With comment by Sargent Shriver, Yves Congar, Thomas Altizer, Bishop John Wright, Leslie Dewart, Karl Rahner, Paul Goodman, and more than 70 others. With discussion questions.

MEN AND NATIONS

The Church in the Modern World — Problems of Special Urgency

With comments by Sidney Callahan, John F. Cronin, Joseph Dillon, John Egan, George Higgins, Walter J. Ong, Mary Perkins Ryan, Bishop James P. Shannon and more than 60 others. With discussion questions.

Available

For use with lay apostolate groups (CFM - YCM - YCS), CCD classes, parish societies, discussion groups, Newman clubs, religion classes in Catholic schools. With discussion questions.